THE
UNRAVELING

My Story of Faith, Forgiveness,
and a Family Restored

Judi Logan

Aurora Corialis Publishing
Pittsburgh, PA

Printed in the United States of America

Edited by: Renée Picard, Aurora Corialis Publishing

Cover Design: Karen Captline, BetterBe Creative

Paperback ISBN: 978-1-958481-06-6

Ebook ISBN: 978-1-958481-07-3

Advance Praise

"In a world filled with pain and resentment, *The Unraveling* delivers a powerful message that forgiveness is not only important but essential for our own well-being. This book dives deep into the concept of forgiveness, exploring its significance and the transformative impact it can have on our lives.

"By reading this book, readers will learn that forgiveness is a painful process but one that ultimately liberates us from the shackles of bitterness and resentment. Drawing inspiration from biblical scriptures, the author emphasizes the necessity of forgiveness and its profound connection to love and compassion.

"As someone who understands the importance of forgiveness, I can attest to the life-altering power it provides. Through personal anecdotes and experiences, the author demonstrates how forgiveness, coupled with faith in a higher power, can restore and uplift even the most shattered aspects of our lives.

"*The Unraveling* leaves readers with a final positive message: forgiveness is not merely an act of absolution but a transformative journey that leads to personal growth, healing, and the ability to live a fulfilling life. With God by our side, the author reminds us, all things are possible, and restoration is within our grasp.

"This book is an important read for anyone seeking liberation from the burdens of unforgiveness. It provides valuable insights and guidance on how to embark on a journey of forgiveness, allowing us to experience true freedom and embrace a life filled with love, joy, and purpose."

Rich "DJ Riddler" Pangilinan
Award Winning Producer, Artist, DJ, Radio Personality
Houston, Texas

———

"Each of us has a unique story, but the beauty of this book is that after all the heartache Judi faced in her life, her story is framed in redemption. God's redeeming power is so evident throughout these pages. He took a childhood that was marked by questions, deception, and confusion, and turned it into a beautiful testimony of clarity and confirmation. *The Unraveling* will be a beacon of hope for those who long to see the broken places of their lives restored. I believe many will be encouraged by the powerful message in this book, and I pray it gives them the confidence to seek restoration in their circumstances as well."

Sue Willis
Founder, Executive Director of Beyond Survival Ministries, Inc.

———

"Judi's journey of self-discovery in the midst of emotional abuse, trauma, and rejection provides readers a unique opportunity to examine their own stories and explore a pathway to healing through faith and forgiveness. Through Judi's story, we're invited to face and acknowledge our own hardships and secrets hidden among our own kin—and recognize we are not alone in family drama and trauma.

"*The Unraveling* is not only one Filipino woman's testimony of God's redemption and goodness, but also a call to action for us to dispel the lies we've been led to believe to make us feel less than, or an outcast. No matter what culture or ethnicity you come from, there's something for all of us to glean from in this beautifully written book."

Sydni Goldman
Media Personality & Producer

———

"*The Unraveling: My Story of Faith, Forgiveness, and a Family Restored* is an inspiring book that delves into the depths of pain, resilience, and ultimately, redemption. In this captivating account, Judi takes readers on a journey through her darkest moments, where she felt abandoned by God and struggled to find her place in the world. With vulnerability and grace, she shares her experiences of enduring hurtful words, uncovering a long-held family secret, and the healing power of faith.

"*The Unraveling* is a testament to the enduring strength and the transformative power of God. Judi's words resonate with readers, leaving them with a renewed sense of hope and a deeper understanding of the true meaning of forgiveness. This book is a must-read for anyone seeking inspiration and a reminder that even in the darkest times, there is light and restoration awaiting those who are willing to take a leap of faith."

Nathan Miller
Lead Pastor @ Champion Christian Center

———

"Judi's story is one of hope and restoration. You will find the love of the father, his forgiveness, redemption, and God's sovereign plan for your life as you read these pages. Judi's life is a testimony that nothing is lost with God."

Joie Miller
Pastor at Champion Christian Center, Author, Founder of Elle Women's Ministry, Host of The Joie Miller Podcast

———

"From the first few pages, this book really tugged at my heartstrings. I felt deeply for what this child went through while searching for her true identity. Several times, I felt like I wanted to rescue her from the mistreatment she faced; however the thread of redemption throughout this book is so powerful and satisfying.

"It was a joy to read how broken people and situations were restored through God's love and unending mercy. This book is a must-read for anyone who is feeling hopeless, those who need a gentle reminder that nothing and no situation is too hard for God to turn around."

Sarah Kapis
Emmy Award-Winning Writer and Director of Beyond Survival Ministries, Inc.

Unraveling – To investigate and solve or explain something complicated or puzzling. To resolve the intricacy, complexity, or obscurity of; clear up or unravel a mystery.

To unravel is to acknowledge and grieve what has fallen apart to allow God's goodness to unfurl. God meets us in the spiraling, unraveling our plans—and us—into something new.

A caterpillar must give up its old way of life to become a magnificent butterfly.

By unraveling, I have become the me I was meant to be.

Dedication

First and foremost, I'd like to dedicate this book to my Heavenly Father. Without Him, I would not have a story of hope, love, and restoration. I thank God every day for a second chance at life and for all the blessings and favor He has bestowed upon me.

Secondly, I dedicate this book to my husband, Chuck, for being by my side every step of this journey. You are my solid rock! And to my children Jacob, Bella, Hannah, Jeremiah, and Zeke for loving me for who I am and not judging my past. For being such awesome children! Thank you for encouraging me to push through. I love you all so much.

Finally, to my family and friends who are so dear to me, thank you all for your love and support.

And to all who read this book, I pray that you feel the love of God woven throughout these pages and into your hearts.

No Longer Slaves

By Bethel Music

You unravel me
With a melody
You surround me with a song
Of deliverance
From my enemies
'Til all my fears are gone.

I'm no longer a slave to fear
I am a child of God.

From my mother's womb
You have chosen me
Love has called my name
I've been born again
Into Your family
Your blood flows through my veins

You rescued me
So I could stand and say
I am a child of God.[1]

---

[1] Excerpt from the song "No Longer Slaves." Bethel Music. "No Longer Slaves." *We Will Not Be Shaken*. Bethel Music, 2015.

You Chose Me

By Bella Logan

In this endless world that you created
Out of every single living creature
You chose me

Even though I make mistakes
And take your miracles for granted
You chose me

Looking for man's approval
When you've already given me yours
It's all I really need
Yet I continue to look for more
You chose me

Infinite planets in your universe
You decided to place me in your world
Though I am with fault, and far from perfect
I don't deserve it
You still think that I am worth it
You chose me

Mama Who

By Hannah Logan

Mama who was like shattered glass
Who was hurt
Who was broken

Who is strong
Who is tough as leather
Who is kind, smart, and important
Who smells of apple pie

Mama who makes yummy sizzling bacon
Mama who takes care of five children
Mama who makes me feel better

Who loves crepes for dinner
Who works harder than anyone
Who makes everybody laugh
Who takes care of others

Mama who loves everybody

~~*

The names in this book have been changed to protect the family.

Table of Contents

Foreword

By Heather Shriver Burns

Have you ever met someone who oozes the joy of the Lord? The type of person you can't help but feel lighter, more hopeful, and more joyful around? If this person is going to be there, you know you're guaranteed to have a good time. That's Judi.

I remember it like yesterday, attending my first volunteer meeting for Beyond Survival Ministries where Judi and I met, as core team members. From the minute I met her, I knew there was something extra special about her. As a business and life coach, I love getting to know people, hearing their stories, and learning the divine assignments God created them for. As we talked, I found that Judi and I have a few things in common besides our love for Jesus, such as our love of good food!

While at a certification training we attended, Judi and I were both craving Chinese and decided to grab lunch together. I was excited to learn more about this woman who always has a smile on her face and has an unusually selfless servant's heart. It was the first time we got to have quality one-on-one time, and that day, my intuition was confirmed. Judi shared her testimony as we drove to and from the Chinese restaurant. I remember gasping when she shared parts of her story. *Who knew?* As I tried to process her childhood and the twists and turns of her life, it was hard to wrap my head around how someone who

i

had been through so much pain and trauma was so full of love and joy.

Judi's story is a reflection of what 1 Peter 1:6-7 tells us.

So be truly glad. There is wonderful joy ahead, even though you must endure many trials for a little while. These trials will show that your faith is genuine. It is being tested as fire tests and purifies gold—though your faith is far more precious than mere gold. So when your faith remains strong through many trials, it will bring you much praise and glory and honor on the day when Jesus Christ is revealed to the whole world.

They say hurt people hurt people. What is also true, though, is that loved people love people. Judi's story is a beautiful testimony of how the love of our Heavenly Father can change everything. Judi's love for life and love for others is a direct reflection of the love she has received. She had every opportunity to allow her circumstances to make her bitter, but she chose to allow God to make her better.

When we allow Jesus to meet us in our pain, comfort us, and free us from the lies of the enemy, anything is possible. Judi's life story gives hope to anyone who wants God to turn their trials into triumphs and traumas into a testimony of His love and promises. I don't know what pains you've endured or what trials you might be going through, but what I do know is there is joy ahead if you open your heart to receive all God wants to give you.

The Bible says every person is made in God's image and that before we were in our mother's womb, He had a plan for us. The enemy hates that you and I were uniquely made for a divine purpose! So much so that he roams around like a roaring lion trying to kill, steal, and destroy us so we never fulfill the calling on our lives. Why? Because when our lives reflect the goodness of the Creator of this world, the Kingdom of darkness loses ground.

I'm so proud of Judi for writing this book, *The Unraveling*. It's like a kick in the teeth to the enemy reminding him that she is the head and not the tail, she is above and not beneath, and he has already been defeated by the blood of the Lamb and her powerful testimony!

After going through my own traumatic loss in 2018, God showed me the enemy isn't after my stuff. He's after my identity, and if it's tied to stuff, sometimes he will go after those things, too. Judi's story reveals exactly the same thing. The enemy was after her identity from a very young age and continued to try to rob her of Truth and the promises of God throughout her life.

What has the enemy tried to rob you of?

It's no secret: the enemy is after your identity, too. He knows if he can get you to believe you're not who God says you are and God is not who He says He is, you will never reach your destiny and fulfill your purpose and calling. The enemy would love for all of us to stay stuck in our pain and not allow

God to redeem our stories so we never have a testimony that tells of His goodness.

Judi's story is inspiring and nothing short of a miracle. It's a real life example of how we don't have to believe the lies we've been fed and can transform our lives when we exchange those lies for Truths. If you're looking to be encouraged, challenged, and reminded of who you were created to be, *The Unraveling* is going to be like honey to your soul. I pray that her story inspires you as much as it did me and, after reading it, you know how very much you are loved and have always been loved.

Heather Shriver Burns
CEO & Founder of Seek First CEO
www.heathershriverburns.com

Introduction

When I was in my darkest moments, I thought that I was all alone. I felt like even God had abandoned me, when in actuality, He was holding me even closer than I could imagine. God's grace and mercy is fresh and renewed every day for us because He loves us so much. And we belong to Him, and no one can ever take that away from us. He looks at you and me and says, "I love you with an everlasting love and You belong to Me."

In Isaiah 43:1-4 reminds us...

This is what the Lord says, HE who created you, Jacob, He who formed you, Israel:

"Do not fear, for I have redeemed you; I have summoned you by name; you are mine.

When you pass through the waters, I will be with you;

and when you pass through the rivers, they will not sweep over you.

When you walk through the fire, you will not be burned;

the flames will not set you ablaze.

For I am the Lord your God, the Holy One of Israel, your Savior;

You are precious and honored in my sight."

Do you remember that poem "Footprints in the Sand"? I was in eighth grade, when one of my friends showed this poem to me. I thought it was nice but did not really pay attention to it much until recently, when it dawned on me how true that poem was. Even before I really knew who God was, even before I knew that I could have a relationship with Him, He already chose me and made me His. All I did was cry out to him, "God, if you are real, make tomorrow a better day." All along I thought I was alone, and when I thought He could not hear me, He was in fact holding me and carrying me through the pain and darkness.

"Sticks and stones may break my bones,

but words will never hurt me."

I remember hearing the other kids in the playground saying this back and forth to each other. I bet they never considered the meaning of what they were actually saying. I'm not even sure where this phrase originated from, but whoever made it up, I don't think they thought twice about what they were saying either. In the physical sense, yes, sticks and stones can break bones, but words can't physically hurt you on the outside, they are not tangible. What this old childhood idiom should really be saying is:

"Sticks and stones may break my bones,

but your words will always haunt me."

Although words cannot be felt physically, they often leave a mark. Over time, they become like ghosts that linger in our minds and infiltrate our emotions throughout our lives. Words may be unseen, but they carry great power! Especially when they are hurtful words that come from the ones you love most. They have a much greater impact than any stick or stone that can be healed in time. Hurtful words, when not properly addressed, can fester, and consume you. "Death and life are in the power of the tongue." (Proverbs 18:21)

Words flung my way throughout my childhood certainly hurt more than I ever thought they would. They impacted me then, and this continued into adulthood.

Those words were whispered in the shadows, sadly by family, those who I thought loved me unconditionally, and for something I didn't even do. Something I was born into.

Those words hinted at a secret that I would spend decades unraveling, researching, and finally healing as God walked beside me. Had there not been divine intervention, my story could have ended in death.

When I search the depths of my memory bank, one feeling always surfaces, no matter the occasion I'm recalling. For a sizable portion of my life, I have felt out of place, like I didn't belong. I simply did not fit in. Have you ever felt that way? It's not easy, but if I've learned anything over the course of a life filled with lies, deceit, degradation, and shame, there's one person who always calls you His own. My story is one of faith and forgiveness, of strength and sorrow, and of a family torn apart by a secret that no one dared to speak of. Words that ripped at my heart led me to call out to God. This is the story of how He took me on a journey of giving my fears and frustrations completely over to Him, and how He restored to me all that was lost… and He chose me to mend the bond.

Allow me to share with you a little riddle:

A child has three sets of parents,

None of whom have ever been divorced (and NO, it is not a cult!).

This same child is the eldest, the middle, the youngest, and an only child, all at the same time.

Is this even possible you ask? Ponder that for a moment.

Chapter 1: Who Am I?

As far back as I can remember, I always felt out of place, different, like I did not belong. Have you ever felt that way? Have you ever felt as if you have fallen into the big blue ocean with your eyes wide open, looking up into the vast waters, and then felt yourself slowly sinking to the bottom of the abyss? You raise your hands and stretch up as high and as hard as you can, but the light of day diminishes as you sink deeper and deeper into the waters. As you gaze up, now with a tiny sliver of light left, you can faintly see the shadow of a small boat on the surface of the water. You open your mouth to scream for help, but it's pointless, no one can hear you now. No one can hear you drowning in your sorrows, drowning in your own cries. The darkness is now closing in at a rapid pace. You don't struggle to get out, you just start to conform. Accepting the inevitable death. This is where it ends, no more struggling.

Just as you're ready to give up, you faintly see a hand reaching down into the water. You're afraid. Is it real or imagined? Is it a façade? Should you reach up to grab the hand and hope that He will save you from self-destruction, save you from demise? Do you feel that you are so far away that you cannot grab a hold of Him? The outstretched hand jolts your lifeless body as it makes contact. Hope is revived. Suddenly, you realize you can survive.

You will survive.

I am living proof that God is never too far from you. All you need to do is reach out and grab hold of His hand. He will save you and take care of the rest. Your life is safely and securely in the hands of your Creator. Even as you gasp for air on the surface, He is there. Right next to you. Your rescuer.

Do you trust Him? I did, even before I knew Him.

I was born in the Philippines on October 29, 1973. I came to the United States when I was four years old with my Lolo (Lolo means "grandfather" in my native language, Tagalog). We were the last two of the first half of my family to migrate from the Philippines.

I don't remember much of my childhood, only a few distinct events remain etched in my memory. The first one was when my Lolo was going to run errands in the city and I wanted to go with him, but he would not allow me to go. When he got on the bus, he saw me crying at the window, feeling sorry for myself. He must have felt so bad for leaving me that he asked the bus driver to stop the bus and wait for him as he went and retrieved me.

My Lolo loved me very much—I would even be so bold to say that I was his favorite. You might not think that is a remarkably interesting story, but you'll soon understand why an act of kindness can take up such precious space in my memory.

The second thing I remembered about the Philippines was when I was about three years old or so, my Uncle Neil (who we called "Papa Boy") hung me upside down in a sack as a punishment because I wasn't behaving. I felt like I was hanging so high up in the ceiling, when in fact, he was just holding up the sack with his hands. Funny how your mind can play tricks on you.

And lastly, I remember someone sending me a lot of money to buy clothes and shoes. My Lolo took me shopping at a popular store called SM Market in Manila. I felt like a princess walking out with so many new dresses and shoes! Honestly, I'm not sure why I distinctly remember those three occasions, but I do know that I held a special place in the hearts of those two men.

In 1977, my grandfather and I left the Philippines and headed to Chicago, Illinois, where other members of our family were already living. My grandparents, parents, sister, aunts, uncles, and cousins all lived in a big black and white house. It was a tight fit, but that's how we liked it. We slept on the floor, couches, beds...whatever was available. I did not know any differently and did not pay much attention to the dynamics of my big family. All I knew was that we were in a new place, a new house, a new country, and we were all happy living and being together again.

My grandparents had nine children; Linda (my mom was the eldest), then came Cacio, Ronnie, Aurora, Elsa, Neil, Zierah, Melody, and Olivia. Then there were 26 grandchildren. Rather quickly, I faced my first challenge: learning to speak English. I knew nothing as I was coming into the States. I remember my sister and cousins making fun of me because I couldn't communicate well with them. English is tricky! But being around all my cousins made it a bit easier to learn and speak more fluently. After a while, I got the hang of it and started doing my best to fit in.

Out of the 26 cousins, my position fell in the middle: the youngest of the older half, but the oldest of the younger half. I always played with and helped take care of the younger cousins. I guess that's why I love children myself. A few years after arriving from the Philippines, my parents did something that changed the course of my life: they packed up their things and headed south, to Sugar Land, Texas. There it is sunny and hot, just like the homeland, but don't let that picture of warmth fool you. My time there was anything but warm and fuzzy. At first, only my mom and my dad moved because they didn't like the cold Chicago weather. Plus, it was difficult for my mom to walk in the winter months, due to her having polio in her feet. My sister, Eve, and I stayed behind in Chicago and were raised by our grandparents, aunts, and uncles.

I was very attached to one of my aunts, Tita Aurora ("Tita" means Aunt). She took particularly good care of me after my parents left. She was always there for me and treated me with genuine care. However, my time with her was cut short because a few years later, the summer after the fifth grade, my sister and I were uprooted and moved to Sugar Land to live with our parents, where we were to start sixth grade.

You would think that after so many years of missing your mom and dad you'd be excited to finally reunite with them. That was not the case for me and my sister. We were both afraid to go to a new place and live with new people. Yes, they were our parents, but they had not raised us, and we felt like we hardly knew them. We did not want to leave what was familiar to us, what we were used to in our formative years. We did not want to leave our grandparents, our aunts and uncles that raised us, or our cousins, who were like our sisters and brothers. At the time, I was only 11, my sister Eve was 12, and we both feared the uncertainty in this big change. There were a lot of adjustments, challenges, and changes we all had to endure together. I'm sure it was a difficult adjustment for my parents as well. Because of our large family, they never had to be responsible for anyone else but themselves. They came to the States to live the "American Dream," to save and provide a better life for their family. Suddenly they found themselves living with two pre-teens, trying to raise them as best as they knew how. It was now just the four of us. I am sure they were somewhat afraid too.

My sister and I were always close, but we became even closer in this new place we now called "home." Our parents were extremely hard workers, and exceptionally good at saving money. My mom was an accountant, my dad an engineer. They also had several other businesses: a remarkably successful wholesale watch company, a decorative blinds business, and an accounting/bookkeeping business. Having these businesses was what they'd dreamed of achieving when they left the Philippines. A few years passed, and like a typical family with teenagers, there were plenty of ups and downs. Unbeknownst to me, this was the beginning of all my woes.

When my sister and I moved to Texas, we felt as though we only had each other. We were kind of afraid to talk to our parents because we really did not know them anymore. As the years went on, I started to notice that things were shifting, and not in my favor. My sister would get special treatment and was favored by my mom. For example, if I wanted to hang out with my friends, the answer would always be "no!" But if my sister asked, she would always be allowed to go, and only then would I be able to go too. Eve was the studious, quiet type who mostly stayed in her bedroom studying. I was more outgoing, always wanting to get out of the house and be a social butterfly.

My mom was much stricter with me and would tell me, in Tagalog, that I wasn't good enough, I wasn't smart enough, that I laughed too much, I was ugly and stupid, and that I would never amount to anything. She would constantly remind me of how smart my sister was and that she was going to be a doctor and even marry a doctor someday (which she did). Later in my life I learned that in the Book of Proverbs 18:21 in the Bible it says that "the tongue has the power of life and death." And that is so true! The impact of words, whether good or bad, is so powerful.

Sticks and stones...

It seemed like my mom took some kind of pleasure in comparing the two of us. She would ask me why I wasn't more like Eve. She was particularly good at playing comparison games and would continually give me a hard time about something, no matter what it was. I never really understood why she did that, or why she would say those awful things to hurt me but not my sister. My mom seemed to always take her anger out on me, whether it was a difficult day at work or if she was just tired. I was in my early teens at this point. As with all teenagers in this season, I was trying to discover myself. I was trying to understand who I was as a person. Then, I had my mother, of all people, telling me I was worthless. My life had no value, no meaning. And this abuse continued throughout my teenage years.

My dad on the other hand was a quiet and kind man. He pretty much followed my mother's lead and agreed with everything my mom would say and do. Maybe it was to avoid fighting. I never really saw or heard my parents fight before. I would just notice that they weren't talking to each other from time to time or that my dad would make jokes and my mom would return harsh comments and that would be it. I remember one time my dad surprisingly spoke in a very harsh tone towards my mom for yelling at me. He said in a stern voice, "Why don't you just leave her alone?" It took me by surprise that he stood up for me. Maybe he just got tired of her picking on me, or maybe he felt bad for me. Whatever it was, I was sure thankful that day.

In January 1989, the year my sister turned 16, my parents bought her a brand new, sleek, navy blue Toyota Celica sports car! Rolled right out of the dealership, it was a beauty, and it was fast. She even had a cotillion, a coming-of-age party. It was a huge party, almost like a wedding. Don't get me wrong, I was happy for my sister. Of course, like any child, I could not wait for my 16th birthday, in hopes of having a lavish party and getting a car just as my sister did.

October finally came around, and it was my sweet 16th birthday. I woke up that morning and looked outside, excitedly! I was hoping to find a new shiny car with a big red ribbon in the driveway—but when I looked outside, my heart sank. There was nothing... no new car, no car at all. No cotillion, not even a party. I believe we just went to dinner that night. I was devastated. I figured that I wasn't worth getting a new car, or I wasn't important enough to my parents to have a cotillion thrown in my honor. It wasn't a money issue for my parents, either; they were successful and had plenty of money. The statements I kept hearing from my mom were starting to feel like the truth: I just wasn't good enough, and I'm worthless. They didn't love me enough for them to shower me with the same gifts and love as my sister. At least that's how I felt and that's what was playing in my head. I was a disappointment to my parents; they weren't proud enough of me to show me the same kind of love and affection they did for my sister. This always bothered me and boggled my mind.

After moving to Texas, all the years leading up to that day, my mom verbally, mentally, and emotionally abused me almost daily. It continued to escalate through my junior high and high school years. I could not understand how a mother could love and spoil one child and hate and abuse the other. I kept thinking whatever she was feeling toward me was my fault. I must've done something so terribly wrong. I blamed myself for all the guilt and all her anger, for all the abuse she was doing to me. The weapon of words cuts deeper through the heart than any weapon that causes a laceration to the body. I was deeply wounded. It must be my fault; I must have done something wrong to her that she hated me so much.

Given that I felt like it was my fault, I thought I could fix it. I would frequently look for ways to try to please her, but my efforts were drowned. I would seek her approval but never get it. I thought that she hated me because I wasn't as smart and as studious as my sister, that I wasn't as pretty, or that I was too loud. I loved to laugh at almost everything and anything, I was a joyful child. My Tita Melody even nicknamed me "Joy" because I was always a joy to be around, and I loved to talk to and entertain people. I remember my mom telling me one time that I laughed too much and that I shouldn't do that because it was not "ladylike." I perceived her mission in life was to knock me down and keep me down.

I often wondered: if she loathed me so much, then why did she even have me in the first place? Why was I even born? I doubted myself; then I started to hate myself. I thought maybe she was right, that I was no good, that I was never going to amount to anything, that I was irrelevant, devalued! I believed, at this point, that I was so brainless and hideous, no one would want me. She found ways to remind me of these things, so I started to think that she was onto something. That's when the lies started consuming my thoughts.

I was living a double life. In school, I was well-liked by my peers and teachers. I was fun to be around; I made lots of friends and belonged to various groups. I would even dare to say that I was one of the popular girls—whether in a good or bad sense, people knew who I was. I was on the track team, French club, math club, drama club, and student council. I was president of my varsity choir where I competed in University Interscholastic League (UIL) Solo and Ensembles and won every time, either first or second place. UIL is an organization that creates rules for and administers almost all athletic, musical, and academic contests for public primary and secondary schools in the State of Texas. It is the largest organization of its type in the world, so it was a pretty big deal for me. I was even a homecoming sweetheart for our homecoming court. I participated in many clubs and activities and got decent grades. One year, I entered the Miss Teen Filipino Texas beauty pageant. My mom did not support me on it and told me I would never win, but I did! I won! Winning the pageant launched my modeling career. I modeled for various malls, did commercials, and was in many musicals and plays. During my modeling career, a Japanese magazine wanted to fly me to Japan to model for them. Of course, my mom did not allow me to go. She shot that dream down, and I waved the opportunity goodbye.

Although I didn't have her approval, I wanted it. With everything my mom said I couldn't do, I would find ways to prove her wrong. I wanted to show her that I was somebody, that I could be successful too. That I was important and that I mattered. I craved her approval, her acceptance, her love. I yearned for it. I just wanted her to love me and see me the way she saw my sister, Eve. I wanted to be loved. I wanted to be seen. But no matter what I accomplished, no matter how good I was, I was never good "enough." I wanted her love.

Don't we all want to be loved? Isn't it natural to seek the approval of the ones we love most? To try to please them? I am sure we all look for that, one way or another, especially from our parents. We all yearn to feel special, to be loved, to be wanted, to belong. Still, I could not figure out what I was doing wrong. I felt the abandonment settling in. The loneliness. The humiliation. The shame. The rejection. One innate human desire is to be accepted. It gives us a sense of self-worth and self-image. Self-confidence. At home, I had none of that.

In a devotional she wrote, actress Romy Downey once said: "You matter and those around you matter. It's human nature that we all want to feel like we belong. Like we matter. We all want to be seen and heard." Growing up, I've often wondered if this saying was true, "When you don't feel accepted, God accepts you."

Prayer

God, thank You for never giving up on me.

I am so grateful that Your promises endure forever.

Nothing is impossible for You,

And every good gift is from You.

I will not fear people or uncertain circumstances,

Because I know that You go before me.

You are always with me, and it's You alone that I trust.

In Jesus' name, Amen.[2]

---

[2] The prayers at the end of each chapter were collected by the author along her journey and have been impactful for her, so she was moved to share them. They are from the YouVersion Bible app. https://www.bible.com/app

Chapter 2: Lifeline

While I was in school during the day, I lived this fun, happy life. I was thriving, I was loved, and I felt secure. But when I came home, it was a whole different world. As soon as my mom came home from work, she would be mad at me for some reason I didn't understand. I would always get the wrath of whatever was bothering her that day. I was constantly walking on eggshells. I cried myself to sleep every night. I just couldn't take the mental and verbal abuse anymore! It was a vicious cycle. I felt like I was going insane, my mind felt like it was going to burst! At night, as I lay in bed, I would cry out, "God if you are real, please make tomorrow a better day. Please don't let mom be angry with me anymore." I would repeat this crying and begging, until I fell asleep. Every. Single. Night. This was my constant plea to God. I remember reading a book in the sixth grade called *Are you There God? It's Me, Margaret* by Judy Blume. That's what I felt like too, asking, "Are you there God? It's me, Judi."

I didn't even know if there was a God. I wasn't sure if He existed or if He heard me at all when I asked: *Are you real?*

I read in Romans 10:14:

But how can they call on Him to save them unless they believe in Him? And how can they believe in Him if they have never heard about Him? And how can they hear about him unless someone tells them?

It's not enough to have an awareness of God. It's not enough to have the knowledge of God. After all, the Bible tells us (in James 2:19 and Mark 1:23-24) that even the devil knew God. If this is the case, then what is it that we need? To experience God, we need to have a genuine, intimate, and intentional relationship with Him.

I grew up in a Catholic church and did all the Catholic things. I went to Sunday school, had my First Communion, and had my Confirmation Day. I had studied and knew of God and Jesus and Mary. But I didn't really know if any of them were real, like real people. I didn't understand what it meant to have a relationship with Him. I never knew that you were allowed to have your own Bible. I thought it was only reserved for the priests, because it was too sacred for us to have one. I always prayed the rosary to Mother Mary and all the various saints for different things. I did not honestly know how to pray. I heard someone say once that prayer is simply having an honest conversation with God.

When I would go through challenging times, I would just call out to God. "If you are real, please make tomorrow a better day." That was my call, my cry for help. That was my prayer. I wasn't sure if He was going to answer me, but I kept calling out in desperation. I would bury my face in my pillow, crying and crying. I didn't know what else to do. I felt helpless, hopeless. This was the start of my journey and, unknowingly, the start of my relationship with my Heavenly Father, my God.

I never knew that we could be so close to God that we can hear Him, feel Him, and sometimes smell the sweet fragrance of the Holy Spirit, until later in my life. I never knew this when I was younger—yet, I still cried out to Him, hoping He would answer me one day. I had nothing else. No one else to turn to. So, I figured, what have I got to lose? Possibly, there is more to gain. Later in my journey of life, I found out that this is what they called "faith." Hebrews 11:1 says, "Now faith is the substance of things hoped for, the evidence of things not seen."

When I would wake up in the mornings, the day would start off well at school, until I got home. I would be anxious, anticipating my mom's arrival from work. Would she be in a good mood today? Or would the psychological and emotional abuse start all over again? Anxiety was on high alert.

I was confused, lost, and broken. My mind was exhausted. You can describe me as "a shattered glass," fragile and broken into many pieces. Was God real or not? Was He playing games with my emotions too? One minute my day would be good, then that evening, it would be horrible. I remember talking to Him, my face buried in my pillow, bawling, and screaming, softly enough so no one in the house would hear me... but loud enough that God could. *God! Where are you? Can you hear me? Do you see me? Help, I'm suffocating! Answer me!* I thought, if only God could hear me, if only I could scream at the top of my lungs... until I fell asleep.

This went on for many years. There was so much pain. I was consumed with feelings of rejection, isolation, loneliness, and guilt. Resentment, brokenness, and helplessness were closing in. I was losing hope and I didn't know what to do. I kept this to myself, I kept it all in. I knew that if I told my sister, Eve, she

15

wouldn't understand what I was going through. She had it made, after all. She was the favorite one and she could do no wrong. I felt that I had no one to talk to, no one to confide in. I felt all alone in my mess.

I believed that no one else had this kind of mess, just me. No one else could possibly be going through what I was. Everyone else's life looked fine from the outside. During the course of life, I learned that everyone, no matter what their background or socio-economic status, can look fine on the outside, but on the inside, they are just as broken, in the same amount of pain and hurt, or even worse than me.

In some form or another, we all wear masks to disguise our pain. We parade around in our daily lives like life is a big masquerade party. Every day we try to look our best, post about the best stuff on social media, and talk about the best things that are happening. But when we sit down and truthfully look at ourselves in front of a mirror, remove our masks behind closed doors, and search deep down inside of us, it's all quite the opposite. We live in a beautified, embellished, fallen world.

The rejection had finally reached a tipping point. If I couldn't co-exist with my mother, I just wouldn't exist at all. I hated myself, I hated not being happy. That's when I tried to commit suicide several times, doing different things to get rid of myself. In my heart, I believed that this was the answer. I honestly believed that no one wanted me, that my life had no value. This statement rang true: I was worthless.

16

I remember the first time I mixed up several bottles of pills and took them all at once. I felt dizzy and drowsy. I thought that was it. As my eyes closed, I had hoped I would never wake up. I slept an entire day and a half, but then I woke up disappointed. Another time, I tried cutting myself, just to feel a different kind of pain, because the pain in my heart was so overwhelming. I could not bear it anymore. Once again, desperately wanting to end it all, I was sure my life would be over this time. On the contrary, I was wrong. Recalling yet another time, I was driving over a hundred miles per hour, zigzagging on a major highway as if I were in the *Indy 500*. It did not matter to me if I caused a major car accident involving others. I just wanted to die. I wanted the pain to stop. I know now that this was very selfish of me back then. I want to remember these demons no more.

This was one of the darkest moments in my life. I wanted to end it all because I didn't think or believe that my life mattered. Fortunately, my attempts failed each time. At that point, I had no idea that there was a real enemy out there trying to get me, like the grim reaper. And I do not mean my mom. I am talking about Satan, the evil one. The enemy had been out to get me since day one. There is a real enemy out there, hunting you down. John 10:10 says: "The thief comes only to steal, kill, and destroy"—in other words, the enemy will devour you any way he can, especially in your mind. The "thief" can be anyone or anything sent by Satan to derail you from the good plans that God has for your life. But God! God said otherwise. John 10:10 doesn't stop there. Jesus says, "I have come that they may have life, and have it more abundantly." Here, Jesus ensures me that I can have a life full of joy, full of His goodness, His grace and mercy. God saved me from destruction. I can reclaim what the enemy tried to destroy: my life.

A friend of mine once said, "all it takes is a beautiful, fake smile to hide an injured soul and they will never notice how broken you are." Living this life is not easy, especially if you don't know God. When you are going through tough times or when life doesn't seem like there's hope, the answer is not to turn to violence. The enemy convinces us that suicide is the answer to all our problems. We are but a mere thought, no one will miss us. Or let's numb ourselves with drugs and alcohol or anything else we can think of to fill that void. No, my friend. Not any one of those things can fill the void, nor are they the right answers. They are all lies! The only thing the enemy can do is confuse our heads with negativity and deception. On the other hand, the God of the universe, our Creator, our Heavenly Father, all He wants to do is heal our minds and hearts. He wants to fully heal your wounds.

Turn to the One who can take every pain away, the One who can get to the root of your problems, the One who can give you freedom and make you whole again. The One who will give you life and life more abundantly (John 10:10). It is that easy. You don't have to change who you are or get yourself together to come to Him. God says, come as you are. "Come to me, all you who are weary and burdened, and I will give you rest," (Matthew 11:28). Perhaps C.S. Lewis says it best: "God doesn't want something from us, He simply wants us."

Coming to God changes us from the inside out, the world changes us from the outside in. You don't have to live a lifetime of compromising who you are, and you don't need to define yourself with what the world says you must be or what you must have. If you define yourself with the truth of God's Word—who He says you are—then you no longer need to compromise anything but only stand firm in what He says. Stay resolved and you will walk in victory and not shame.

We are created for more than we can ever imagine. We are children of the most high God. And we are to overtake this world of the enemy. The devil knows this all too well. When we are aware of our true identities and to whom we belong to, it destroys the plans of the devil. If you know the Bible, at the end of the day, God wins and conquers all, He throws the devil in the depths of hell and throws away the keys. And we, the believers of Him, will be taken up to Heaven and live with God, happily ever after. Sounds too good to be true, right? Oh, but it *is* truth.

We believe our self-image and our self-worth are rooted in what others think about us. We want and crave the approval of people, of the world around us, just as I craved my parents' approval. This is what the enemy wants you to think and keep you bound to. Therefore, we think we are not good enough, that we simply aren't enough, or that we will never get there. The reality is that we do not need the approval of others; we simply need God's approval. He says that: You. Are. Enough! God will affirm you and seal your priceless value. All we need is the audience of One.

I questioned all this growing up because my relationship with God was distant. I did not know it then, but God had bigger plans for my life.

Prayer

God, You are worthy of all my adoration!

When I look back on my life,

I realize that You have always been there.

Even when I felt alone, even when I couldn't feel You,

You were at work behind the scenes.

Since the beginning of time,

You have done great things.

Thank You!

In Jesus' name, Amen.

THE UNRAVELING

Chapter 3: Doomsday

Growing up Catholic, we would go to church every Saturday evening or Sunday morning. During Mass, an older lady and I would lead worship and sing the prepared songs in front of the congregation. Instead of being a proud parent, my mom would laugh at me and make comments like, "Why are you even up there? No one can hear you. Maybe you are just lip-syncing it," or she would say, "You sound like a chicken cackling." Do chickens even cackle? I wasn't sure why she didn't want me up there. I couldn't comprehend the concept of her not being proud of me either. The lady I was singing with and the organist would say that I did a wonderful job and that I have a beautiful voice. I know I didn't sound bad. I was in the varsity choir throughout junior high and high school and had won many awards statewide. In her opinion, I was not good enough, but oh, how I longed to hear accolades from my mother.

Around this same time, as a teenager, we had been attending Filipino charismatic prayer groups for a few years. We would rotate meeting at different friends' houses. It was potluck style, so we would all bring various dishes to share. We fellowshipped and ate dinner together first. Then someone would play the guitar and lead us in singing and worship, before diving into the Bible study for discussions. If I'm recalling correctly, I believe we would meet every other week; eventually, our prayer groups became like family.

I still remember that dreadful day vividly, like it was yesterday. It was a humid Saturday, and the sky was a light gray, because it was raining hard outside. It was early evening, and we were getting ready to go to one of those prayer meetings. I must have been 16 or 17 years old—I don't quite remember, because I've tried to block out that painful memory.

Earlier that day I had asked my mom to wash my favorite jeans to wear to the prayer meeting that evening. She was in one of her moods again. As the day went on, I took a shower and was getting ready to go to the prayer meeting. I came to find out that she did not wash my jeans. I was terribly upset with her. We fought; she was angry and yelling at me. Now, I urgently had to find something else to wear.

I had no idea that asking her to perform this simple task would send her over the edge. I guess my mom could not hold her tongue any longer. She had a burning secret inside her that had been pent up for many years, and the utterance of it would change the trajectory of my life forever. What happened next would permanently be etched in my mind. It continues to play in my head like a broken record.

My mom and I had been butting heads all afternoon. As we sat in the car, waiting for my dad and my sister in the driveway, the woman I had known and called my "mom," turned around abruptly, and burst out in Tagalog, "Hindi ka naman anak ko!" The familiar words of my native language stabbed me deep in the heart like a knife. "You're not even my child!" There was a sudden catastrophic climate change in the atmosphere. "What! What are you saying?!" I cried.

24

Then she doubled down, this time in English, and said, "You are not my daughter!"

That statement destroyed my world. I felt like I was tossed and turned upside down. Wait! What? What did you just say?! If you're not my mom, then who is? Who am I? I was so confused.

Have you ever received news that you were completely unprepared to hear or digest? This was it. I felt like the wind was knocked out of me. I couldn't breathe. How my heart sank to the floor. Much like Niagara Falls, a rushing flood of tears came down my face. Sadness loomed over me. Surprisingly enough, at the same time, I breathed a sigh of relief. It was as if a heavy burden had been lifted off my shoulders. That's when it all came to focus. A surge of memories instantly downloaded; all the abuse started to make sense. I was not going insane, thinking a mother could not love her own child, could not love me. Or that everything I was experiencing was my fault; it was NEVER my fault. All the blame and shame that I took on was not even mine to carry.

In my mind, I finally understood the truth of why she was so bitter and angry toward me. I did not belong to her, but she was forced to raise me. She resented me, she resented her parents, and she resented my biological mother. Actually, she resented the predicament she was in. She had taken all her frustration, anger, hatred, and bitterness out on a young, innocent little girl. None of what happened was my fault. I was the product of something sinful, but it was NEVER my fault. Part of my wondering was finally answered: I was not hers.

That's why she treated me the way she did. Every frustration, every anger, every ounce of bitterness should've been aimed at someone else. I was just a convenient target.

It all made sense.

I was crying and crying when my dad and my sister got in the car. My sister asked me why I was crying. In between the heavy breathing and sobbing, I managed to tell her what our mother had said. "Mom said that I'm not her daughter, and you're not my sister." Eve began to cry in disbelief. In the midst of my grief and confusion, I managed to hold her hand and tell her that no matter what, we will always be sisters. She loved me because I was her only sibling, her baby sister.

That's when my dad piped up. He looked at my mom with disappointment and said, "What did you do?" The cat was officially out of the bag and there was no turning back. We rode in silence the rest of the way to the prayer meeting. Yes, we still went, as if nothing had transpired. When we got there, my sister and our friends ran upstairs to one of the bathrooms, and I told them what had happened. Everyone was in shock, but they were supportive. They didn't judge me or look at me differently. That was a relief. Later that night, when we got back home, each of us went to our separate rooms and did not talk about the earth-shattering secret that had been unveiled just hours before.

Allow me to recap that for you in case you missed it. The first set of parents I had was not my parents; biologically, they are my aunt and uncle, and Eve is my cousin. In this family, I am the youngest. Although I grew up calling them "Mom" and "Dad," it was in title only. So, if they weren't my parents, then who were? The answer to that question tore me up. Who did I belong to?

Prayer

God, You are my refuge and strength,

And my help in times of trouble.

Even when I face difficult situations,

I will not fear because You are with me.

You cover me and protect me.

You go before me to fight my battles – and You always win.

Nothing is impossible for You, which is why I can confidently say

You are my help when I am in need.

No matter what I face today, I will place my hope in You.

In Jesus' name, Amen.

Chapter 4: To Whom Do I Belong?

Sometime the next day, I called my Tita Aurora, my favorite aunt. She is my grandparents' fourth child, and my mom, Linda's first sister. She was the one I always ran to and called for help, every time my mom yelled at and abused me. My Tita Aurora was the one who was always there and mostly took care of me, before we moved to Texas. She is truly a kindhearted, gentle, understanding, and generous person. I always felt safe talking to her.

I remember when I was eight or nine years old, I got severely ill. I felt as if I were dying. Many details are hazy, but I do recall lying in bed and my Tita Aurora was sitting beside me, putting a cool towel on my forehead to lower my temperature. In that moment, I whispered to her, "I wish you were my mom." She asked me why, and I said, "Because you take good care of me, and I know you love me." I don't remember what she said after that, I think I had fallen asleep.

Recollections like this came rushing back to me as I got up the nerve to tell her about this recent revelation. I conjured up the courage to ask her the question that had plagued me since the night before: "Do you know who my parents are?" Turns out, the question had a simple, yet profound answer. One that I was, once again, not ready to receive.

In that moment, my Tita Aurora confessed that she was in fact, my biological mother. What a relief! No wonder she was the one who took care of me before moving to Texas, and no wonder she was so kind to me for all these years. I thought back to that time I told her that I wished she was my mom. I could only imagine her holding back her tears and her tongue in that moment. I am sure she had wanted to tell me the truth but couldn't because she was bound to secrecy.

When I asked my Tita Aurora what had happened, she finally told me the truth, or so I thought. It was the biggest secret in our entire family; it was the "forbidden secret." All my mom's siblings and their spouses knew about me, who I really was, and who I belonged to. They were all sworn to secrecy, because of the disgrace and shame it would have brought to the family.

When a friend or relative would say, "You look so much like your Aunt Aurora!" all the aunties and uncles would laugh and look at each other, in hopes that no one would breathe a word. They all knew but didn't dare say a thing, for fear one of them would expose the truth. They didn't even tell my cousins. It's funny how small things come into focus once you have a view of the bigger picture.

I recall how one of my aunties got upset with me one day, and she blurted out that I was a "bastard child." I was young when that happened, but it stuck out to me. We didn't have smartphones or computers back then for me to look up the meaning of "bastard child," and we didn't have a dictionary around either. Out of curiosity, I asked my Tita Elsa the meaning of a "bastard child." She blew it off and said, "Never mind her, she does not know what she's saying." So, I took her word for it and didn't think about it anymore.

Now that I knew who my real mother was, I still had another burning question: Who was my biological father? The answer to that question would unearth years of pain, guilt, and shame for her, but I had to know. As I talked to my Tita Aurora, I asked why she didn't just keep me, raise me, and take care of me. Why did she give me to her eldest sister, Linda? I had so many questions.

She proceeded to explain to me that, when she was 22 years old, and still living in the Philippines, my grandfather kept an awfully close eye on her as she was growing up. He was extremely strict with her because she was an incredibly beautiful young lady. Regardless of how diligent he was in protecting her, she was somehow snatched from their home, kidnapped, and raped. Fortunately, she got away from her attacker, and her family was able to recover her. Days after, the police found and arrested the man who hurt her and brought him to trial. During the proceedings, she had a traumatic nervous breakdown. It turned out that rehashing the entire ordeal was just too much for her to handle. She was hospitalized and could not continue the trial. At that time, in the Philippines, if you had money, you could pay off the judges and lawyers to drop and close the case. This is exactly what the perpetrator's family did. They took advantage of the situation, so nothing came of the trial, and charges were dropped.

I know what you're thinking... but no, I was NOT the product of that rape.

Many years after this, she found and married a man who is just as kindhearted and generous as she is, who accepted everything that had happened in her past, including me. I call him my Tito Antonio (Tito means Uncle). When they got married, he loved and treated me as if I were his own daughter.

Prayer

God, when I face situations beyond my control,

Help me to choose joy and hope.

Fill me with a sense of your presence that is

Greater than any of my present difficulties.

No matter what I go through, I will rejoice

Because You are my Savior,

And my strength comes from You.

In Jesus' name, Amen.

THE UNRAVELING

Chapter 5: The Secrets That Made Me

My grandmother had nine children. Growing up, she had a favorite cousin who had eight children. They were a big, close-knit family. The two first cousins were the best of friends: best cousins. Their children, who were second cousins, were remarkably close as well. They would frequently visit each other's houses, play all day, and sometimes sleep over. As they grew older, some would stay at my grandparent's house, because their school or college was closer in proximity than their own house. This was the epitome of a close-knit family.

One day, the family was completely torn apart, and all hell broke loose. Relationships were severed, and the love that had existed between the families morphed into trauma, heartbreak, animosity, and wrath. This was the Hiroshima kind of bombshell that caused both families to part ways, never to see or speak to one another ever again.

Back when the whole kidnapping and rape incident happened to my biological mom, the entire family was devastated. Both families banded together to get through the tough situation. One day, one of the older male cousins saw that my mom was not herself and he decided to take her out to cheer her up. This is where it gets a little tricky because there are always two sides to the story. Regardless of how it truly happened, the bottom line is, he took advantage of her vulnerability. Things happened that should not have happened. Because of that, I am the product of that incident. I came into this world. That's what drove a wedge into the close-knit family.

When I became aware of my conception story, I felt impure and filled with so much shame. I could almost feel the sinful act of the flesh that had occurred. I felt the depths of hell. I was already so broken from the emotional and psychological trauma I had experienced from Linda; now, I was even more embarrassed and ashamed of where I came from and how I was conceived.

Once again, I had so many questions about how something like that could possibly happen. And more questions about my biological father. Tita Aurora told me that, at that time, she really didn't care about herself. She felt no one cared for her. After the whole experience of being kidnapped and raped, she was completely numb. She had no feelings and no respect for herself. She too was so broken that she didn't care what happened to her anymore. She was feeling exceptionally low about herself, a feeling that I can identify with. She never consented to her cousin, my father, taking advantage of her. Nothing mattered to her anymore. In that moment, I was curious for her to continue, but she didn't really want to talk about him or talk about what had happened any longer. This was still a sore spot in her life that she had buried and was trying to keep from being resurrected. I got up the nerve to ask her one final question before she completely shut down: where was my father? She told me that he had died a long time ago and that I didn't need to look for him. So, I let it go. Her answer made me feel like I never knew him, so why would I bother asking what he was like? He's already gone anyway.

My (biological) mother did offer some details about the earliest moments of my life, but they were disturbing to hear. She said that when she found out she was pregnant with me, she hated herself. She hated that she got pregnant by her own cousin. She was ashamed and humiliated. Not only was he family, but he was much older than her and was already married with two children of his own. He had committed adultery, and together they had produced an illegitimate child. My mom slowly opened up about the grueling nine months that followed. She did not want to be pregnant. She had no desire for me. The sinful baby that was now growing inside her was enemy number one. She said that she tried everything she knew to try to get rid of her pregnancy, to remove the shameful evidence that trapped her in this predicament. She would purposefully try to starve herself to death, so I too would starve and be depleted of the proper nutrients needed to develop. Other attempts, like hitting her stomach or harming herself somehow, became her mission. She did whatever she could think of to hurt or damage her unborn child conceived from sin that she now had to carry.

Abortion clinics were not really a known thing back in the Philippines either. The family was strict Roman Catholic, so you just didn't do that anyway. She admitted that she never even had any check-ups or doctor visits until it was time for her to give birth. Even her parents hid her away from the public to avoid embarrassment—first because she was pregnant and not married, but also because of who the father is. That would have been a disgrace to an affluent family in the Philippines.

Tita Aurora (which is what I still call my biological mother, even though "Tita" means "aunt"), said that all the attempts she made to abuse herself to get rid of me were unsuccessful; I was unharmed. When it was time for her to give birth, she was afraid of what I would look like, because of the damage she may have caused. When she heard me crying, she knew my lungs were strong. And when she first laid her eyes on me, she said I had come out perfectly healthy and whole. She inspected every part of me that she could. She made sure I had ten fingers and ten toes. She told me that her eyes were fixated on me; a beautiful, unharmed baby, and that she had instantly fallen in love with me. She was thankful that none of her attempts to destroy me touched me at all. No damage whatsoever. I was a survivor, even from the time I was in my mother's womb.

God's hand of protection and favor was on my life from the very beginning. I am reminded of Psalms 139:13-16, where it says,

For you created my inmost being; you knit me together in my mother's womb. I praise you because I am fearfully and wonderfully made; your works are wonderful; I know that full well. My frame was not hidden from you when I was made in the secret place, when I was woven together in the depths of the earth. Your eyes saw my unformed body; all the days ordained for me were written in your book before one of them came to be.

God has always been with me.

After giving birth, it was not her choice to give me up, but that was her only option at the time. She had no say in the matter. She was 23 years old at the time. Unmarried and not mentally stable, she was not in the right state of mind to be caring for an infant. All decision-making power was stripped away from her. My grandparents forced her to give me up to her eldest sibling, Linda, who was already married, working, and established.

At the same time, my new "Mom" and "Dad" (who were really my biological aunt and uncle) were forced to take me in, give me their last name, take care of me, and pretend I was their own daughter. I'm sure that's where all the resentment, guilt, and hatred started. They were forced to take the responsibility of taking care of an infant who wasn't even their own and who they certainly didn't want. On top of that, they had just had their own baby girl, my cousin/sister, Eve, nine months earlier. To make matters worse, NO ONE was ever allowed to breathe a word of it. It was a forbidden topic. My true identity was more than a secret; it was a burden.

Prayer

God, thank You for giving me hope and a future.

Thank You for reminding me that pain

And grief won't last forever.

There is more to my story.

When I feel overwhelmed by my suffering,

Please remind me that You are with me,

And that You will remove all of my pain one day.

In Jesus' name, Amen.

Chapter 6: Surviving the Secret

I was in high school when this all came out—and when it did, I couldn't face my peers. Although they didn't know what had happened, I was so ashamed on the inside, struggling to conceal it from the outside. It was too much. It was all so overwhelming: how I was conceived, that I wasn't even wanted by my real mom initially, not being wanted by Linda, and my real dad being dead. Basically, I was rejected from the start by everyone. I belonged nowhere and to no one! I felt abandoned and orphaned.

Now I had a SECRET of my own. I did not want anyone to know who I really was. I was afraid that my sister was going to start telling our friends that we weren't really sisters and that instead, we were cousins. I was afraid that she was going to tell them that I was a product of rape and that I was fatherless. A bastard orphan, an illegitimate child. It was at that moment that I finally understood what my aunt had said to me in the past, why she had called me a "bastard child" because that's what I really was. The labels we put on ourselves. The lies we begin to believe. The unimaginable secret with which I was plagued.

I was terrified that my friends would find out the truth about me. No one ever really talked about family situations or dynamics back then; it was taboo. I believed that all my friends had perfect, "normal" families and that all of them had their own moms and dads. I never really knew of anyone being adopted because no one talked about it. I didn't want my peers to find out my secret.

I can recall my parents' (Linda and Carlos's) 25th wedding anniversary. We had a huge celebration for them at a very nice hotel. We had relatives from all over the States travel to Texas to celebrate the occasion. We were all dressed so fancy. Before dinner began, the officiating priest came up to say a prayer over the food. He began by thanking all the guests on behalf of my family. Then for whatever reason, he said that I was the adopted daughter of Linda and Carlos. I'm not sure where he was going with this, but I felt humiliated! I was so embarrassed that I ran out of the ballroom. He made me feel like I did not belong to the family, that I had no place there. I felt like I could no longer show my face. I ran outside crying. My boyfriend at the time chased me outside to make sure that I was ok. He knew that it was a punch in the gut for me. Although the secret was out, I wasn't ready for it to be publicly announced like that. And to hear someone else say it made it too official. I was still in the healing process. My heart took another blow.

It was the worst feeling I had ever felt, not to have a sense of acceptance, safety, or belonging. I felt like I was going to implode. I was lost and alone. I had nothing, I had no one. Just because the truth had come out, it didn't mean everything was better at home now. It in fact got worse; the psychological trauma continued. Linda would tell me that I was a mistake and that I should've never been born. The abuse got so bad, I wanted to run away and die. My sister and I drifted apart. I felt the walls closing in on me once more. I had no one on my side. I felt that now that Eve knew the truth about us not being sisters

42

anymore, she was no longer obligated to be my sister. Ugly words and hatred passed our lips. I remember Linda and Eve would have closed-door conversations that I was not privy to. To this day, I'm not sure what was discussed behind those closed doors, good or bad.

My mom never really trusted me with anything. I know that I wasn't her real daughter, but to be treated more like an outsider... I hated it and now I hated my life more than ever. I felt ostracized. I was quickly spiraling, sinking into a sea of shame, fear, guilt, hopelessness, and depression. The enemy was winning. So many secrets to hide. Shhh! Don't tell anyone. I felt like I was losing myself. Losing my identity. God, please! When is this going to end?

Advancing ahead, I did manage to finish high school with very few people knowing that my sister, Eve, and I weren't sisters. We were exactly nine months and twenty days apart. Our friends would wonder about that but then would laugh it off. I vowed to myself that I would leave someday and never return to Texas. My childhood memories were just too painful. After I graduated high school, I moved out to Bolingbrook, Illinois, where my real mom, Tita Aurora, my stepdad, Tito Antonio, and my half-sister, Anne, lived.

To recap: My second set of parents turned out to be my biological mom, Tita Aurora, and her husband, my stepdad. In this family, I am the eldest. I have two younger sisters. One in heaven and my half-sister, Anne, we have the same mom–Tita Aurora.

I left my secret life behind in Texas, and I moved in with them. I wanted a fresh start as I ventured off to college. My desire was to major in international business and marketing with an emphasis in logistics. I love to travel and explore new places. I figured no one knew me in Illinois. A new place, a new identity, a new me. I wanted to leave any baggage behind as I embarked on this new journey. Life was a little better. I felt like I could breathe easier. Linda was still involved in my daily life. She didn't want me to move to Illinois; she wanted me to stay and help her around the house, because my cousin/sister, Eve, had moved out too. She wasn't ready to be an empty nester.

She still disapproved of any decisions I made. Of course, my stubborn self would try to prove her wrong. Like the time I wanted to purchase a high-rise condo in downtown Chicago. I was 23 years old, and she still had the same effect on me. She didn't want me to do it. She insisted that I would not be able to afford it. When I moved to Illinois, Tita Aurora and Tito Antonio bought me a car, but soon after, I was in an accident and the car was totaled. I used the money I received from that as a down payment and eventually purchased the condo of my dreams by myself. I was single and young living my best life in downtown Chicago in my new high-rise condominium. I was on the twelfth floor, looking over the city from a distance. I lived in my condo, went to college full time, and worked downtown full time. I walked everywhere and was in the best shape I could be in. I was living the life I wanted and proving Linda wrong again. But no matter how happy I was, or how well I was doing as a young adult, it still wasn't good enough for her. Even then, I was still looking for her approval and love. I just wanted her to love me.

Our relationship was a never-ending rollercoaster, always up and down. One minute she loved me, and I was in her living will. The next minute, she was angry with me, and she didn't love me, and I was out of the living will. One day my pictures would be displayed around the house, then the next all my pictures would be taken down. This psychological warfare continued for years. When I got married, she said that my marriage would only last for seven years. Now, what kind of person would say a thing like that? Again, I proved her wrong, my husband and I have been married for 22 years and counting. But even as a married woman, I still craved her approval.

Prayer

God, thank You for redeeming every part of my life.

You are a hiding place for me, and

You preserve me from trouble.

When I run to You–I am safe.

Thank You!

Today, please show me how You are protecting me.

Guard my mind and my heart.

Please continue to preserve my life.

In Jesus' name, Amen.

Chapter 7: My Special Some "One"

I had been dating different men, looking for love in all the wrong places. Sound familiar to you? So, cliché, right? When I moved out to Illinois for college, I not only left Texas behind, but I also left my boyfriend of seven years. There was a moment in time when I believed that he was my knight in shining armor, so, we decided to stay together and try this long-distance relationship out. At the same time, I was going out with other men. I'm not proud of that. Bouncing from one guy to the next. I did not have any serious relationships—I was just looking for the "one" who would love me.

In the summer of 1998, I met my future husband—only I didn't know it yet. Chuck Logan and I had worked in the same office together, but I never officially met him until my last day of work with that company. It was surreal, just like the movies: I looked up from my cubicle and saw him from a distance. Everything seemed like it was moving in slow motion. I asked my best friend, Jessica, who worked with us, who he was. She was the human resources manager at the time, so she knew all the employees there. He was tall, nicely tanned, and handsome. You can tell he worked out in the gym a lot. (I am a sucker for tall, muscular men. I guess it makes me feel secure in their arms.) "Is he new here?" She proceeded to tell me his name and said that he'd been working there for three years. She also told me that he was "off limits" because he had a girlfriend. How could I have missed him? I was a social butterfly, and I knew pretty much everyone in the company.

It was a Friday, and I was ready for the weekend. I went about my business that day. Sometime in the late afternoon, Chuck came to my desk holding a flyer for a party. We'd never spoken before; then out of nowhere, he showed me the flyer and asked if I was going. I said, "Well of course I am, it's my going away party!" I explained to him that it was my last day of work there and that I was transferring to another company. He said, "Ok, I'll see you at the party then."

Later that evening, we saw each other at the party. He brought his friend who was 6'9" tall. He introduced me to him. We were intoxicated and partied all night with our friends and coworkers. Long story short, Chuck later admitted to me that he was trying to set me up with his tall friend, but his friend said that I was too wild for him and that he could have me. This became a running joke about how we eventually got together. We both broke up with our significant others (and I severed all ties with the other guys as well) and decided that we wanted to date more seriously.

We went out on a few more dates. I can recall the first movie he took me to; we watched *Armageddon*, starring Bruce Willis, Liv Tyler, and Ben Affleck (my favorite actor back in the day). The theme song for the movie, "I Don't Want to Miss a Thing" by Aerosmith, became our theme song. We both didn't want to miss a thing! We enjoyed each other's company. Chuck and I are 10.5 years apart, but we liked similar things and had so much to talk about. Our conversations would last for hours, and they were filled with laughter. He always made me laugh.

We never wanted to get off the phone when it was time to go to bed. I remember we would go back and forth saying "you hang up, no you hang up first!" This would go on and on for a bit until we found something else to talk about. Sometimes, we would just stay on the phone just to hear each other breathe, until we'd both fall asleep.

During the day, while we were at our separate workplaces, we would send each other exceedingly long emails and talk about all sorts of topics. This was before text messaging was invented. We were very spontaneous, happy, and free to be ourselves. We loved cuddling on the couch watching NASCAR racing and UFC fights. Our favorite sitcoms were *Friends* and *Seinfeld*, and we would even watch the cartoon *South Park*.

One of my criteria for dating was that you either knew how to cook and cook well or you would let me order off a menu because I was particularly good at doing that. Well, it turned out that Chuck is an exceptionally good cook. I remember early on in our dating; he would cook me some gourmet meals, like steak and lobster! Wow, did he win my heart! After seven months of dating, he asked me to move in with him. Yes, the carnal sin of living together before marriage! I never thought this would happen to me. I thought that I would not live with a man without being married first. I remember one day I slept over at his place, and he got called into work. I was getting ready to leave, when he said, "Why don't you just stay here, since you'll be coming back again later when I get home from work." "You trust me to stay here without you?" I asked. Without hesitation, he said, "Of course, why not?" This made a significant impact on me, that someone that I had known for only a few months, trusted me enough to stay alone in his apartment.

Trust was a huge factor for me—not only in relationships but with everyone I meet. After all the deception that I've been through, for him to trust me like that, touched my heart. I didn't even know if I could trust myself. This was new to me. I instantly felt safe and loved. This is what I was missing in my life growing up. So, when he asked me to move in with him, I said "yes." Mind you, this was BC (Before Christ… that is, before I had Christ in my life); before I knew what the Bible said about fornication and living together before marriage. Funny thing is, Chuck was already a born-again Christian who had backslid. (When a Christian backslides, it means that they relapse into their pre-Christian ways of not following Christ's example of living.) When Chuck was 15 years old, a friend of his had taken him to church. He was so touched at the service that he accepted Jesus Christ into his heart and started instantly living for God. A couple of years passed, and he became a deacon at the church, proclaiming the gospel. He was on fire for the Lord!

After a while, when a Christian is not continually in the Word of God, the world and the flesh take over. When he was in his early 30s, Chuck fell away from God and backslid into worldly things. When we met, we were both living in the world and not for God. We had our share of drinking and partying excessively. It got so bad that one night of clubbing, we both had one too many drinks and couldn't remember how we drove and made it home in one piece and had woken up the next morning to a charred pizza in the oven. God was surely looking out for the both of us.

We got married on August 18th, 2000, in Naperville, Illinois. It was a gorgeous, sunny day. We had a traditional Filipino Catholic wedding, and the cathedral was beautiful. My color scheme was a light seafoam green. We had a huge wedding entourage consisting of a matron of honor, maid of honor, bridesmaids, junior bridesmaids and their male counterparts, a ring bearer, cord bearer, and Bible bearer, and the list went on. We both came from large families and had lots of friends. So many friends and relatives traveled from all over the place, both domestically and internationally. We had a little over two hundred guests! It was a huge wedding!

Our reception was held at Walter Payton's Roundhouse. The building is the oldest limestone roundhouse in the United States and a historic landmark. It was an old, abandoned building that housed and repaired steam locomotives and railroad cars back in the day. The pride of the Chicago Bears and the famous pro football Hall of Famer, Walter Payton (along with other partners), purchased and renovated the entire building. They converted it into a restaurant, brewery, cigar bar, and banquet hall. It even housed the Walter Payton Hall of Fame Museum. The place was phenomenal! We had an open bar, and they served a seven-course meal; the drinks and food were excellent. The DJs we hired were so good that everyone was on the dance floor the entire time. It was amazing!

Not too long after we got married, the thirst for alcohol and the days of partying left our systems. That desire quickly and permanently abandoned us. Instead, the desire of knowing God more instantaneously entered our hearts. My husband taught me that it was okay to have your own personal Bible. At the time, I thought it was only reserved for priests. He also taught me that there was more to God than just what you see on the surface. Accepting Jesus as your Lord and Savior and developing an intimate relationship with God is what moves heaven and earth. Chuck is truly knowledgeable and is an excellent teacher of the Bible. I will be forever grateful to my husband for sharing the gospel, teaching his faith, and leading me to Christ. My salvation story is simple, I wanted more of God, and so I made a covenant with Him. I accepted Jesus Christ as my Lord and Savior in September of 2000. I saw myself in a whole different light. I have a new identity now in Christ Jesus.

In 2 Corinthians 5:17-21, Paul teaches that being "in Christ" results in a person becoming a "new creation!" The old life is gone; a new life has begun! God has provided salvation and reconciliation for us through the sacrifice of His son, Jesus Christ. We now have a new identity as a son or daughter of God. I am a child of God. The flame in Chuck's heart began to burn brightly again—only this time, we were doing it together.

Within 13 years of marriage, we had five amazing children: Jacob, Isabella (Bella), Hannah, Jeremiah (JT), and Zechariah (Zeke). My husband and my children know about the special dynamics of my three sets of parents and all the moving parts involved. They understand, love, and respect every one of them.

Prayer

God, thank You for Your unfailing love toward me.

Every day You show me mercy and grace

Beyond anything I could ever deserve or imagine.

Thank You for the love, hope, and eternal life

I have access to because of You.

All praise belongs to You alone!

In Jesus' name, Amen.

Chapter 8: Deception Much?

In 2015, we took a family vacation over Father's Day weekend to Finger Lakes, New York. The crew consisted of me, my husband, our kids, my mother (Tita Aurora), and my stepdad (Tito Antonio). My youngest son Zeke, who was barely two years old at the time, burned the palm of his hands on a smoldering hot glass fireplace. We took him to the emergency room at the nearby hospital. We were there for hours. The doctors diagnosed him with deep second-degree burns on his tiny hands. They were wrapped up in so many bandages and all I could think of was comforting him.

Naturally, in the moment, I was more concerned with the welfare of my baby boy than recognizing the importance of the day — it slipped my mind that it was Father's Day. I didn't get a chance to call Linda's husband (my dad, Carlos). That did not go over well with them. When I finally had a chance to think and got in touch with him and Linda, I was told that I was ungrateful. Despite the fact that Tita Aurora called them earlier to explain what had happened, they were still upset with me for not calling. This incident caused a separation for three years. We did not talk or see each other for all that time. Believe it or not, I did miss them. Even after all we had been through, I still considered them my parents and I would always keep them in my prayers. Don't get me wrong, they are good people, they did provide for me, albeit with strings attached. Their provision and "love" were not the unconditional kind. I wasn't a part of their life plan; I was forced on them, and they did the best they could. I was an added burden to their little family that they had not expected.

Ephesians 6:12 tells us, "For we are not fighting against flesh-and-blood enemies, but against evil rulers and authorities of the unseen world, against mighty powers in this dark world, and against evil spirits in the heavenly places."

If there's one thing I've come to understand over the years, it is that the enemy will use any means possible to cause division and keep families apart from each other. The hurt feelings are very real. We tend to fall into these traps when our hearts and minds are not guarded by the Word of God. We must remember to allow grace and mercy into every situation, just as Jesus Christ had grace and mercy upon us when He paid the price for our sins on the cross.

In 2004, Papa Boy (Uncle Neil, from the beginning of the story, who had hung me upside down when I was little) passed away. I was incredibly sad because he always made me feel as though I was his favorite. He was kind to me and treated me like his own child. After the funeral service, we had a dinner reception, where so many of our relatives from various places had come to pay their respects. Tita Aurora came up to me and introduced me to a man. She said, "This is your Uncle Miguel." I said, "Hi, nice to meet you." I didn't think anything of it, because when you're a Filipino, everyone is your "aunt" or "uncle," even if they're not blood relatives. So, I thought he was just another "relative."

Then she clarified, "This is your Uncle Miguel, your real dad's brother."

My eyes widened, "Ohhh, ok, hi."

I instantly realized that this is the first relative from my biological father's side that I had met. Although, he told me that we've crossed paths before. All those times my family and I had visited St. Louis to see other relatives, he would see me, but could not approach me to say anything. This was forbidden, as he would have been sworn to secrecy. Then he showed me an old picture of him and his siblings. He pointed to the picture, and spoke some life-changing words:

"This is your dad, your papa." Wow, there he was in the flesh! My father. My uncle proceeded to show me more pictures and that's when I asked him when the photos were taken. His response floored me. He said, "Not too long ago, when we visited him in the Philippines, maybe last year or so." Shock waves surged through my body. I said, "What? Wait a minute, you mean to tell me he is still alive?" He replied, "Yes, he is, and he is strong. I told him about you. I told him how you are married and have a son." I was in complete and utter disbelief! My father was alive and well, after all these years, I thought he was dead! I didn't say anything. Before we parted ways, Uncle Miguel gave me my father's address in the Philippines and encouraged me to write to him. I walked away extremely confused and concerned that this would be the start of a brand-new round of drama and lies in my life.

Just when I thought it was all over, here we were again.

Now I wanted to know why Tita Aurora had lied to me. She had told me in the past that he was dead and to let it go. Another secret unraveled! Can't I catch a break and have some truth in my life? She really didn't have anything to say when I confronted her about it except that she didn't want me to look for him because she didn't want me to get hurt again. Apparently, she was worried that he wouldn't accept me because he had his own family. I couldn't blame her; she was just looking out for me as all good mothers do. She was protecting me.

To recap: My biological dad and stepmom are my third set of parents. In this family, I am a middle child. I have an older brother, an older sister (who is just nine months older than me), and a younger sister.

I contemplated for a while whether to write to my father. An overwhelming sense of rejection and abandonment came over me again. That familiar feeling of panic I know all too well set in, and the questions started coming:

What if he doesn't even want to talk to me?

What if he denies me, denies that I'm his biological child?

What if he thinks that I was a mistake too?

I thought I had been done with all these thoughts and feelings. I didn't want to go through it all over again. The pain was just not worth it.

A few months passed without any action on my part, but I kept feeling a nudge, a gentle push to write to him. Then one day, I finally decided to just do it and see what happened. I wrote to him and told him all about my life, how I was married and at that time only had one child, Jacob. I gave him my address and phone number. I wasn't expecting a return letter, a phone call, or anything. A few weeks later I was looking at the caller ID and to my surprise, it was a phone call from him. I was shocked, excited, and nervous all at the same time. Do I answer the call or just let it go to voicemail? I was hesitant. Fear got the best of me. So many questions were spinning around my head. Two rings, now three. I didn't know what to expect… what he was like? What we were to talk about?

I ran and hid inside my closet and composed myself, then I got up the nerve to answer the call. There I was, after 31 years, finally speaking to my biological father. Just when I thought that he was dead, and no longer in my life, I said my first" hello" to him. A sigh of relief came over me. He sounded so caring and so interested in getting to know me. He was in fact interested in me. I can still recall that moment. I felt like that little girl that was so excited to talk to her papa while he was away on a business trip. It was a feeling of euphoria. Thirty-one years seems like a lifetime. He didn't deny me, he accepted me for who I was, although he didn't know me. The love of a parent was so important to me, since I felt like no one ever wanted me. He finally did.

This is just like the love of our Heavenly Father. He's interested in us, and He wants to have an intimate relationship with us. He accepts us just the way we are. All we need to do is answer that call and say "hello" God, I'm here. Jeremiah 33:3 shows us that God will answer our cries when we reach out to Him. "Call to Me, and I will answer you, and show you great and mighty things, which you do not know."[1]

We talked about a lot of things, mostly general, get-to-know-you things. During our conversation, two details stuck out to me. The first one was that he said to call him on his cell phone only, not the house phone. I found it odd, but I agreed. Second was that he said that he loved me very much. He said the last time he saw me was when I was first born. Another detail that I didn't know. He said that he wished to meet me in person and that one day, we would. For the first time in my life, I felt like I belonged to someone, that I could finally say that I had a dad of my own, that someone loved me and wanted me, that I wasn't forced on them.

I was so happy and proud that day. He called me, and we talked a few more times after that. But I was always curious as to why he didn't want me to call on the house phone. One day, out of curiosity, I decided to call the house phone. Little did I know that his wife, my stepmom, had just recently found out about me. Neither he nor any of his siblings ever told her about his secret past and that he has a daughter with someone else! After all these years, he never told her the secret he'd been harboring. I thought to myself, here we go again with the drama, and more lies. Before I was even born, my life was full of lies, secrets, and deception. Would it ever end? When will I have truth in my life?

Luke 12:2 reads, "The time is coming when everything that is covered up will be revealed, and all these secrets will be made known to all." For me, just once, I wanted some truth in my life, something sustainable, something meaningful.

The phone rang and rang. I was nervous because I didn't know who was going to pick up the phone—then there was her voice, his wife, my stepmom. She said in a stern and firm voice, "Who is this?" I said, "It's Judi. Can I please speak to my papa?" She said, "Who?" I began to repeat myself when I heard shouting in Tagalog in the background. Oh no! Here comes the drama. In the midst of shouting, I heard my papa say, "You'd better be nice to her. Don't be rude." Then she yelled back, "Tell her not to call my house!" This went on back and forth until he grabbed the phone from her.

When my papa got on the line, he apologized profusely for her behavior. I asked him if she knew about me and he said "Yes," but he conveniently omitted that she had just found out recently. We talked for a little bit more, but I could still hear her disgruntled shouting in the background. I did not like what was happening. I didn't want strife in their marriage to be my fault. I wanted to make things right, so I asked him if I could talk to her. He was taken aback that I was interested in speaking to her. It was unsettling to me that she was angry. I wanted to make things right with her.

When she got on the phone, I wasn't sure how to address her, and I sure didn't know what to say. I took a quick breath and said a little prayer in my head. I asked her if I can call her "Tita" out of respect. She said, "Yes." I assured her that I wasn't there to ask for anything or to take anything away from her or her family. All I wanted was a relationship with my papa, as well as with her and my siblings. I told her that I was not a bad person, that all I wanted was to one day be a part of her family too. I even explained to her that I understood how she was feeling and that if I were in her shoes, I'd be frustrated and furious too. I expressed to her that she had every right to feel the way she was feeling toward me, that she was justified.

I felt her anger subside a little. She let her guard down for a moment and started to open up a bit. She expressed to me that she had just found out not too long ago. The unimaginable secret and betrayal were still fresh on her mind. I felt her agony as her voice was quivering, telling me her side of the story. I can imagine myself in her position as she was describing her wounded heart and exasperation toward my papa. Her one true love, the father of *her* children had done the unthinkable and hid it away from her for years. And all she could do was accept it. Everyone expected her to just accept it. Doesn't seem too fair for her, in my opinion. I'm sorry that this happened to her. I wouldn't wish it on anyone. But here we are. I reminded her that what happened was the past, and that neither of us could change it, even if we wanted to. The trajectory of this family tree was already in motion long before either one of us knew anything about it. It wasn't her fault, and neither was it mine. All we could do now is move forward and get to know each other. I wanted to show her the respect she deserved and the love of Christ that never changes.

My stepmother, whom I now addressed as "Tita Betty," was slowly interested in knowing me too. She was just as intrigued by me as I was by her. She started talking to me and asking me questions. She asked me when I found out. How did I know? She also asked if I understood her discontent towards me. I said, "Of course I did." I'm sure she was curious of my feelings too. She was probably wondering: Who is this person I'm supposed to let into my life, into my family? Is it safe?

Overall, I thought the conversation went well. Until later that evening, I learned my perception was completely wrong and that quite the opposite had occurred: they fought even more when we got off the phone. I had to keep reminding myself of Ephesians 6:12: "We are not fighting against flesh and blood, but against powers and principalities of this dark world." The enemy did not want anything good to come out of this; he wanted to continue the destruction he had started. My papa and I didn't talk for a while because I didn't want to get in the way of their marriage. We would talk on occasion and on holidays just to keep the peace in their household.

Prayer

God, thank You for being a constant refuge for me.

I am so grateful that I can always turn

To You in times of trouble.

Whenever I feel afraid, anxious, or depressed,

Help me to place my trust in You alone–

Because You will never abandon or forget me.

In Jesus' name, Amen.

Chapter 9: The Call

Many years passed. On November 9, 2017, I received an urgent phone call in the wee hours of the morning through Facebook Messenger. I didn't answer it right away; I was just barely waking up to start my day. After my morning routine of waking up the kids, getting them ready for school, and driving them down to the bus stop, I had crawled back into bed. I always check my phone to review my calendar and see the schedule for the day. As I was scrolling through my phone, I noticed a notification from Messenger. It was from my Ninang (Godmother) Arianne, who happens to be my papa's youngest sister. She too lives in the Philippines.

I opened the message, and it read:

"Pray for Kuya (big brother) Railey, had a massive heart attack.
Now, at the Philippine Heart Center.
Needs triple bypass. Thanks, and God bless."

I hadn't realized how urgent it was until I listened to the voice message she left on my phone as well. It was a Thursday morning in Pittsburgh, Penn., which was Friday evening in the Philippines. Then I realized that I also missed a couple of calls from my Tita Servidea, she is my dad's eldest sibling/sister. Things had started to feel urgent. My heart suddenly dropped. So many thoughts were going through my mind. Ninang

Arianne and Tita Servidea had both called several times. Was it bad news? I started to cry as I was frantically trying to return their calls but to no avail. So, I texted my Ninang Arianne:

"Ninang, please call me back. What happened to my papa?"

I waited in my bedroom impatiently, desperate for an answer. Something, anything, I just wanted to know what was going on. Did he make it? Is he still alive? *Please someone tell me what's happening!* I had so many unanswered questions running through my head. I was not sure why I was crying so much for a man I barely knew. The tears just kept on coming like a waterfall.

I was crying for my papa, but who was he, really? We only spoke on the phone a handful of times and wrote a letter or two to each other over the course of 11 years. I only saw pictures of him because I didn't have video calling on my phone at that time. I was a little behind on technology. It wasn't enough to form a true bond. I was 44 years old, and I had never even really met my biological father. So why did it hurt so much? Why was I crying so profusely?

I prayed to my Heavenly Father. I said: "Lord, I'm not sure why I'm crying so much for someone I don't even know; someone I've never met before. My heart hurts, Lord. Please keep my papa safe. I want to meet him. I have never met him in person. I want to see him and meet him, while he is alive and not when it is too late. Please keep him alive for me, in Jesus' name."

My Ninang Arianne finally texted me back; she said that she just wanted to let me know. She didn't want me to find out in case the inevitable would happen. Then it would be too late. I didn't even know what to say to her. I felt overwhelmed with emotions. I was crying and crying, and I couldn't process why.

I was consumed with emotions and confused about how I was supposed to feel. The yearning that I've had for so long was overwhelming me. The emptiness that I've felt but wasn't sure what it really was. A piece of the puzzle was missing, a hole in my heart. I couldn't comprehend this feeling, because when I accepted Jesus into my heart and gave my life — me — to Him, He was enough for me. I know I have always felt God's love for me. He is my Heavenly Father. I didn't need another Papa, right? So, I thought. I mean, God is sufficient, my God is more than enough. He fills my void.

As I sat in silence, in deep sadness, my God reminded me that my papa is still my papa. We are connected. The Lord said to me, "You're crying so much for this man, because he is a part of you and you are a part of him, he is still your earthly father. He is the missing puzzle piece that completes your longing." That is why I felt such an overwhelming pain in my heart.

Yes, my God is sufficient, but at the same time, He gives us the desires of our heart. Psalms 37:4 reminds us to "Delight yourself in the LORD, and He will give you the desires of your heart." God filled that emptiness in my heart that I had forgotten about. Growing up, I always wanted a dad to call my own, someone I belonged too. Someone who would also call me *his* daughter with no strings attached. And He did just that;

God fulfilled that longing. Don't get me wrong, I love my other two dads (my uncle/dad Carlos and my stepdad/uncle Antonio). But it's a different kind of feeling and a different kind of yearning to know that you literally *come from* this person. There was a void in my heart that only my biological father could fill, and God reminded me of that desire.

As I was praying and thanking God and crying, all at the same time, I prayed and said this: "God, you are more than enough for me. I want to meet my earthly father. I don't know how Lord, but you do. Please keep him alive for me, heal him, and make a way for me to visit him while he is still alive, in Jesus' name."

I pleaded with my God. I was halfway around the world, feeling helpless, my heart heavy, my eyes and face puffy from crying, and very exhausted at this point. Before I lay back down to try to fall asleep and get some rest, I texted my husband, Chuck, to pray for my papa, because he had just had a heart attack and needs a triple bypass. I told him to also pray for God's provision because I really feel that I need to go and see him right away. He texted back, and I fell asleep.

When I woke up sometime after 11:00am, I got Jeremiah and Zeke ready for their day. As we were eating lunch, Jeremiah noticed my sadness. He asked, "What's wrong, Mama?" I told him to pray for his Lolo/grandfather in the Philippines because he had a heart attack. Later in the day as the other kids got home, I told them as well. My kids are so good! They knew how I felt as I was getting choked up, telling them. They all said in their own ways, "Don't worry Mama, he'll be fine. God is taking care of him, so you can meet him someday." They all hugged me and kissed me.

Thank you, Jesus, for such good, compassionate, and caring children!

I asked the four older ones to do their homework and keep an eye on their baby brother, Zeke. I wanted to lie down again because the stress and crying had given me a terrible migraine. When my husband got home, he saw me sleeping on the couch but didn't want to wake me. I'm a light sleeper, though, so I heard him in the kitchen anyway. From the couch, I reminded Jacob that he had to be at church for worship practice at 7:00pm, and I reminded Jeremiah that he had basketball practice as well.

Chuck heard me. His response was, "I'd like to sleep all day too, you know!" Oh boy, wrong answer! I went ballistic on him. I asked him, how can he be so insensitive? Didn't he care about the news I had just received? I felt as though he didn't even care what I was going through. It was as if what I texted him earlier about my papa wasn't even a big deal to him. I told him that I've been crying all day long and that I had a migraine because I'm so stressed out. So many emotions were flooding in my mind and my heart, I could not even think straight. I was so angry, I just rolled over and tried to fall asleep again. Chuck eventually took Jacob and Jeremiah to their respective practices.

When he came home, he sat next to me and apologized for his insensitivity. He said that he was really sorry about my papa and that, no matter what, we would find a way for me to see him. I wondered how we could afford the trip, though. Where would we get the money? What about the kids, who will take care of them? He assured me not to worry. God always makes a way, especially when we think that there is no way, because with God nothing is impossible. (Isaiah 43:16 & 19, Luke 1:37).

God had a plan all along. What the enemy meant to keep apart, God put all the pieces back together again, just like a puzzle. I called my godmother back and told her that I wanted to travel to the Philippines to visit my father. She said he was ok, waiting to have surgery. He had three arteries blocked, and the lining was very thin in one of the veins. He would definitely need a triple bypass. "Just pray for him."

She was telling me all of this as I was just listening and crying over the phone. And the only thing that came out of my mouth was, "Ninang, I want to see him alive." She said, "Find a way to get here, and once you're here, we'll figure out the rest."

I couldn't just go and see him because his wife, my stepmother, would not be pleased. So, I prayed about what to do. I asked the Lord to make a way because it seemed impossible to me. I had to get a passport and a ticket to the Philippines, which was expensive. Plus, I was afraid to tell my mom (Tita Aurora), that I wanted to go see the cousin who took advantage of her in her frailty. The man she claimed was already dead because she didn't want me to meet him at all.

I talked to my stepdad, Tito Antonio, first, and I told him the situation. I told him that I wanted to visit my papa and get to know him a little, while he was still alive. He understood me and all the emotions I was going through. He was so kind and gracious to me, and he said he would talk to my mom and prep her for me. The next day, I called my mom, Tita Aurora, and told her what had happened and what I wanted to do. She was very calm, and she asked me if this is what I really wanted. I know she was just looking out for me; I know she did not want me to get hurt either by him or his wife. She knew that I'd been so emotionally broken and scarred from my past, that she didn't want me to endure anymore. I pleaded with her, "I have to do this." I needed to fill a gap in my life, and I just needed to meet him before he died. She understood.

Unexpectedly, she offered to pay for my plane ticket. God makes a way when we think that there is no way! The plan was now in motion.

Prayer

God, thank You for protecting me,

And for keeping watch over me at all times.

Because You are always looking out

For the righteous, please show me

How to pursue what is right.

Provide me with more opportunities to draw near to You.

In Jesus name, Amen.

Chapter 10: T-Minus 10...9...8...

Many things happened over the next 10 days between that call and my departure date. The devil was trying to prevent this trip from happening. One thing after another, the enemy kept putting obstacles in front of me to discourage me from going. I know it was the hand of the enemy because God was about to do the miraculous. I wasn't sure what God was going to do, but I knew it was something that the enemy did not want to happen. I focused on the fact that my God is bigger than any of these roadblocks, believing that my God would see me through. Every hurdle the enemy put in place; God combated. "My God will never fail!" (Joshua 21:45).

A friend of mine who was a travel agent found a ticket for me quickly for a decent price with the shortest overall travel time possible. But my passport was another hindrance. It was going to take four to six weeks to return to me, provided there were no hiccups. This was not acceptable, because I was getting ready to leave within the next few days. So, my husband and I hopped in the van with all the kids and drove to Buffalo, New York, because a friend said that you can apply in the main passport office and possibly get your passport that same day. We weren't sure if this would really be possible, but I was willing to take a shot.

We left on a Thursday afternoon, drove to Buffalo, and stayed overnight. Bright and early Friday morning, we went straight to the Buffalo Passport Agency. I went in alone. There were so many people waiting in line. I took a ticket and waited patiently for my number to be called. As I was waiting, I prayed for God's divine intervention and favor on my passport. "Number 58!" That was me. I went to the window with my paperwork and passport photo in hand. A sweet older lady greeted me. "How can I help you?" she asked politely. I explained to her that I was in urgent need of a passport. I proceeded to tell her that my dad was in the hospital awaiting heart surgery and that this would be my first time in 44 years meeting him. She was choked up and teary-eyed. She signaled for me to hand her my paperwork and photo.

Holding back her tears, the nice lady told me how much it would cost and said to come back in three hours. I went back to the car, where everyone was waiting for me, and we went out for brunch while we waited.

Three hours later, we went back to the passport agency. The line was just as long as before. I pulled another ticket. I waited for my turn again. When I got to the window the second time, a different lady showed me a beautiful passport with my photo on it. She told me where to sign, and I paid. Done! I thought to myself, what a relief.

I got back in the car, and we headed back home to Pittsburgh. All I could think was, "God is so good, and His hand is on this journey!" When we got home, I started to pack and made sure that everything was in order. I wrote exceedingly long, detailed instructions for my husband to follow for the next three weeks. I didn't want to interrupt the kid's routine with schooling and activities they had. I wanted to keep it as normal as possible without me there. My husband had asked his boss for permission to work from home those three weeks, and thank God, His favor was on us. Everything was set in motion; everything was going according to God's plan. But the enemy had a plan of his own too.

The enemy thought that he could stop me from what God had planned to do all along. Leading up to the day I was leaving, I did all my last-minute packing, bought gifts for my relatives (we call this "pasalubong," which means "I come bearing gifts"), wrote out all the children's daily instructions, packed my passport, and called my godmother to let her know my arrival time. Everything seemed to be in order until I called the airline to check in and confirm my flight. They said that they could not find my name or my booking information.

I panicked... I was supposed to fly out the next morning! I frantically called my friend who booked my flight for me. She assured me that my ticket was in order. I called the airlines again and gave them my full name, including my maiden name. Then finally, after so many tries of entering my name in numerous ways, the agent found it. She said everything was in order, and I was set for the entire flight, including the connecting and return flights.

Whew! Was I relieved!

Prayer

God, when I'm afraid, I will put my trust in You.

I will rely on You no matter what comes my way

Because You are my source of strength and safety.

You guide me and fight for me.

When I draw near to You,

I have nothing to fear,

Because I know that you are in control–

And You are all I need.

So today, I intentionally choose to trust in You.

In Jesus' name, Amen.

Chapter 11: Destination: Philippines

That Sunday morning, we headed to the airport bright and early. My family went with me to see me off. They were happy for me, but at the same time, they were sad as well, because I've never been away from my husband and children for that long, especially on the other side of the world. It was going to be a long three weeks ahead. I really didn't know what to expect or what I was looking forward to. It was all going too fast. I was going back to my homeland, the Philippines, where it all happened, where I was conceived and born. Luckily, I could still understand and speak our native language fluently.

On November 19, 2017, at 6:10am, I boarded the plane alone. It was United Airlines flight 895, seat 45G, heading to Chicago, Illinois for a connecting flight to Hong Kong with a final destination, the Philippines. I remember thinking: *What in the world am I doing here, getting on a plane, leaving my husband and children, traveling halfway across the world, to meet my biological father for the first time in 44 years?! This is either going to be amazing, or this is completely insane!*

Suddenly, overwhelming feelings of fear and anxiety crept in. The "what if's" were shouting in my head. The volume was almost deafening. *What if my father doesn't want to see me? What if I'm a disappointment to his family? What if I get cold feet and change my mind? I can't just turn around and fly back.* As the plane progressed down the runway, my clammy hands clenched the seat handles. I felt a cold sweat come over me. I took a deep breath as the plane took off into the sky. As I sat there, I just prayed and prayed for God to do the miraculous. For God to do what He does best. I prayed for protection from the enemy in every situation and prayed that I had God's favor and blessings upon me. I kept praying for God's will to be done in this situation, telling him that I would do whatever He needed me to do. I had no idea what He wanted me to do. I had no idea what was going to happen because only my godmother and my cousin knew I was coming. I prayed and prayed until a feeling of peace and calmness swept over me. I fell asleep.

It was a long flight, 22 hours in the air with an hour-and-a-half layover in Hong Kong. When we landed in Hong Kong, we deplaned, and I searched for my connecting flight. All the signs were foreign, nothing in English. I asked an agent where my connecting flight was, but she didn't speak English. Still, she managed to point me in the direction I was to go. I don't remember being afraid. I just knew I had a destination to reach. And a mission to accomplish. I felt a sense of peace wash over me. I know my God was guiding me. I found my connecting flight and waited to board the plane again. It was a smaller aircraft. When it was finally time to board, I found my seat, buckled in, and fell asleep. Final destination: the Philippines.

As the plane was making its final descent, I kept praying that I would carry out God's plan in all of this. Although I knew that I wanted to finally meet my biological father in person, I wasn't sure how he was going to react or how his wife was going to react. My mission was to meet my father, but knowing God's character, He would have bigger plans than just that to accomplish.

We deplaned and I followed the crowd out. I was listening to the people talking all around me. Hearing my native language, I felt comfortable and at home instantly. I was among my people. As I looked around the airport, all I could see was a multitude of Filipinos. All I could think was, "This is where it all began: my birthplace." I got to the baggage claim and retrieved my things. I saw my godmother and met her daughter, my cousin, Zoe for the first time. They greeted me with huge hugs. No crying, mostly joyful laughing. It was as if we knew each other already, and it's just been a while. It was surreal. Zoe drove us to their house. It was a modest two-bedroom, two-story house. The entire street was lined with the same type of building, one right next to the other. As we entered her house, my godmother showed me the bedroom that I would be I staying in. I got settled in and unpacked my things. I was exhausted and jet lagged. After getting situated, I rested for a while.

Later that evening, I met my cousins Jem and Summer. They were also my godmother's daughters and Zoe's sisters. We all went out to dinner at Max's Restaurant—a Filipino restaurant chain famous for its crispy chicken. My cousins wanted to take me there because it's a popular place to eat in the Philippines (they also have locations throughout the United States and Canada). As we walked into the restaurant, the smells were so aromatically pleasing to my senses. I was ready to order everything, although I hadn't seen the menu yet!

The hostess brought us to our table. We reviewed the menu and decided to order fried chicken, fried shrimp, and my favorite noodle dish, palabok. Palabok is a dish made with clear noodles, served with hardboiled egg slices and shrimp, and topped with pieces of crispy pork rind. They give you a few lime wedges to squeeze over the top of the noodles to bring out some extra flavor. It was mouthwateringly delicious! The chicken was super crispy on the outside and so juicy on the inside. It was scrumptious, with just the right amount of spices. They also gave us a small bowl of soy vinegar with garlic sauce for dipping. The shrimp was succulent and just as crispy. Of course, you can't eat chicken and shrimp without some white rice! White rice is a staple dish in the Philippines. All these entrees were equally delicious! My mouth is still salivating as I'm writing this! Oh, how I missed eating Filipino food and how I missed my native land! The servers were genuinely nice and accommodating too.

People in the restaurant noticed that I wasn't a local; I was dressed differently and looked "Americanized." They probably heard me speaking English with no Filipino accent either. I got some looks, not bad ones. Just stares and whispers of "she's from the States." There's a running joke among the Filipinos that when they would try to speak straight English, they would say "nosebleed" after each sentence, along with their Filipino accent. I guess it meant that they were trying to speak proper English so hard that they felt like their nose would bleed. My cousins, my godmother, and I all laughed as they were trying to explain this to me. It was good to be back in my homeland, and good to be with family.

A couple of days passed. I went with my godmother to the Catholic church a few times. The churches were big, beautiful cathedrals. We visited many different malls. The malls in the

Philippines are huge! Most of them are four to six levels high! They literally have everything at the mall. They have your typical stores for shopping, as well as giant movie theaters, church services, post offices, grocery stores, restaurants—you name it, it's probably there. It is so hot in the Philippines that people will literally stay at the malls for hours because of the air conditioning! Most people hang out there all day long. It is a gathering place, and truly an experience and a beautiful sight to see.

While all of this was wonderful, I could not lose sight of why I was there—to reunite with my father. I wasn't on vacation; I had a mission and a divine appointment sent from God. We eventually needed to decide when we were going to make an appearance in my papa's home. My godmother and her sister, Tita Servidea (the eldest sibling) took the lead. They discussed it and decided on a plan of action for how I was going to show up unannounced. First, we went to visit another relative, Tita Connie. I believe she is a cousin of theirs. My Ninang Arianne, Zoe, and I went to her house. She was nice and accommodating. They talked about her coming with us to see my papa the next day.

Plans were in motion and coming together.

The next day, we woke up and got ready. Zoe drove, we picked up Tita Connie, and then we headed over to Tita Servidea's house. I met her husband, Tito Connor. He was a nice man. There was a gentleness and kind spirit about him, and Tita Servidea said that he was a very hard working man. Tito Connor got really sick and passed away about a year after I met him, so I'm glad I had the opportunity to connect with him before he passed. We took some pictures and then left. My cousin Zoe, my godmother, Arianne, my Aunt Servidea, and my Aunt Connie were all with me, heading to my papa's house.

The drive was far, and traffic in the Philippines is quite different from traffic in the States. Good thing my cousin Zoe is an excellent driver; she methodically weaved in and out of the streets. It's a bit crazy and challenging driving in the Philippines Although there are lanes, no one follows them. All the cars heading in the same direction just try to weave in and out of each other. I'm surprised that not many accidents happen. They say that when you've mastered driving in the Philippines, you can drive pretty much anywhere. That's how crazy it is! Not only are there cars and buses competing to merge, but there are also motorcycles, tricycles, and vehicles called Jeepneys. Jeepneys—repurposed old jeeps left by the U.S. Army at the end of World War II—are the cheapest and most popular form of transportation in the Philippines. They are essentially loud and colorful minibuses, with open backs, and passengers just hop on and off as they please. Then you also have people walking in between the vehicles on the busy streets selling drinks and snacks because the traffic is so bad. The people in the Philippines are innovative and do whatever it takes to support their families.

We stopped at Jolly Bee, a popular fast-food chain restaurant, for lunch. This particular Jolly Bee was the 100th Jolly Bee restaurant that opened up in the Philippines. It's kind of like McDonald's in the States. You walk up to the counter, place your order, pay for it, and wait until your order is filled.

We ordered Filipino-style spaghetti with hot dog slices. The sauce has a bit sweeter taste than the Italian spaghetti we're used to. We also ordered palabok with fried chicken, a hamburger-type meat with a mushroom gravy sauce over white rice, and pineapple juice and water to drink.

We received our food, sat down, and ate. We talked, laughed, and got to know each other some more. Then we continued driving for a couple more hours until we reached our destination and parked right in front. There it was, finally: Papa's house. Tita Servidea asked me to stay in the car and told me they would come and get me when they were ready. My three Aunties went to ring the doorbell and my cousin Zoe stayed by the car like a bodyguard, waiting for the "all clear" signal.

Prayer

God, fill me with bold courage

To live for such a time as this!

You have placed me exactly where I need to be

And chosen me for a specific purpose.

Free me from fear and guide my decisions.

I want to live today as Your chosen child.

In Jesus' name, Amen.

Chapter 12: The Encounter

It was so strange that they made me stay out of sight. I wasn't sure what they were doing or what exactly was happening... it just felt bizarre. I had so many emotions building up to this moment.

I couldn't believe I was, in fact, in front of my papa's house! In just a matter of minutes, I would finally meet him. I never imagined this day would come. I was pinching myself, and I was thanking God that my dream of meeting this man, my papa, was about to come true. At the same time, I was a bit nervous and frightened of what would happen next. Have you ever felt that way? The anticipation of something you've been longing for so long, something you've been dreaming about, ties your stomach in knots just waiting to burst.

Suddenly Zoe knocked on the window and opened my door. She asked me to step out of the car. Was this it? Was he standing outside of the doors? To my surprise, it was not him. Zoe introduced me to my younger sister, Rachelle. We said "hello," and we hugged each other as if we'd known each other since birth. It was so nice to finally meet! She said that she's known about me for quite some time. Both Rachelle and our older sister Cathy had been searching for me on all the social media platforms, but they couldn't find me because I didn't have any social media accounts! With five kids to take care of, I just didn't have the time for it.

Earlier that year, in March 2017, my dear, close friend Clara and I had been sitting at a Starbucks along with some other friends. They were scrolling through their Facebook accounts and talking to each other about some of the things that they were looking at. Of course, I had no clue what they were referring to because I didn't have social media. So, then Clara, out of nowhere, literally took my phone and decided to set me up on Facebook. We were all laughing and saying that it was about time I caught up with this century! We pretty much had the same group of friends, so she friended them for me. She taught me the basics of what I needed to know to get around Facebook. I wasn't very savvy on social media as I was new to the whole thing. But I did tell my family that I was finally on it. It's no coincidence how God just orchestrates everything in His timing. He already knew that this moment in time was going to take place. And He already planned and made a way for all of us to be able to connect.

Zoe, Rachelle, and I chatted a bit outside. I kept looking nervously toward the house to try to see what my aunties were doing. Turns out, they had cornered my stepmom, Tita Betty, and were explaining to her that I was outside, waiting by the car with Zoe and Rachelle. They asked her to stay calm and not make a scene so my papa wouldn't get worried and stressed out—an important precaution given his recent heart attack. They explained to her that I had flown halfway around the world to meet my papa and to spend some time getting to know the family.

In a perplexed tone, Tita Betty had replied, "She's here?"

She couldn't believe I was there, right outside of her home. After explaining the situation to her more and reasoning with her, they said she was "calm and good," and that's when we knew it was time. They gave us the "all clear" signal that it was ok to bring me to the front door. She too was peeking out to see a glimpse of me. I saw my papa walk past the front door a couple of times.

Here it was, the moment of truth. I was about to meet my papa! I was shaking and extremely anxious. Zoe took my phone to take pictures and to video the whole experience. Rachelle held my hand and walked me to the front door. With each step we took, my heart hammered harder and harder in my chest with nervousness and excitement all at the same time. She opened the door as I stood beside her. I wasn't sure how to react or what to expect... after all, it had been 44 years! FORTY-FOUR YEARS!

I said a prayer in my head, "Lord, be with me."

As we stood by the front door, Rachelle called out, "Papa, come here, I have a surprise for you." With my heart racing as if it would jump out of my chest, I saw my father coming toward me. This was it!

When he got to the door, he looked at me intently, mesmerized. He placed both of his hands on top of my shoulders. Confused. He couldn't say a word, frozen; he just stared at me, as if he saw a ghost. The moment this was happening, the few seconds that it took place, seemed like a lifetime and it was all going in slow motion. The look of uncertainty in his eyes pierced through mine.

All I could think was, "Here he is; it's really him!" My smile reached from ear to ear. Then I broke the silence and said, "Hi Papa, it's me, Judi."

His intense look broke, and he did a double take. Then, the most special moment of all. He stepped forward and wrapped his arms around me intently. He hugged me fiercely. In between the heavy tears, he hugged me tightly and said, "Is it you? Is it really you, Judi?" I said, "Yes, it's really me, Papa."

It was everything I could have hoped for. Like a scene from a movie, only it was really happening to me! We both cried and cried in disbelief. It was a rushing flood of tears, tears of joy. He was so happy and surprised that I was there in person. The day that he had been waiting for too, to finally hold his long-lost baby girl in his arms. All he kept saying was, "I love you. I love you. I've always loved you!"

I felt this heavy burden that had been weighing him down for so many years finally lift from him. I'm not sure what that burden was. Maybe it was the burden of guilt and shame. Maybe the burden of lies or the burden of keeping up with such a massive secret. Whatever it was, it left him as soon as he said those words to me, "I love you. I've always loved you."

I will never forget the tenderness of that moment. The gravity of a father, at long last, meeting his daughter, and a daughter meeting her father after 44 years, was an unforgettable and beautiful occasion. It was like a fairytale. Oceans separated us for most of our lives, but in that instance, we were as close as close could be. Nothing could keep us apart. Regardless of how I happened, I was his and he was mine. All was forgiven, and the past was wiped clean. Just as Jesus did for us on the cross, we got a second chance. A new chapter in our lives. A new chapter in our story.

When I look back at the video and pictures that captured the experience, it's difficult not to get choked up. You can literally see and feel the love of this God-orchestrated encounter. I can almost hear the music playing in the background. There are no words that can truly describe the feeling of meeting your biological father for the first time. It is, indeed, priceless!

This pivotal moment in time, this experience, was so sweet and so precious. I finally met my papa, someone I longed for, someone I belonged to, who loved me and longed for me as well. Those feelings I will never be able to shake off. I still remember it as if it were just yesterday.

We made our way inside the house to the living room. Tita Betty was standing there. I made my way toward her and gave her a big hug as well. We all sat down, me between my papa and Tita Betty. I held both of their hands as we talked and got to know each other. They complimented my beauty and my smile. I felt incredibly special that day. There was so much love in that room, I really felt like I belonged and that I was home.

They tried to FaceTime my older sister, Cathy, because she was away on a business trip. I was able to talk to her for a bit, but the connection was bad. After a little while, more family came over, including my brother-in-law, Leo, my niece, Ellie, and my nephew, Judd. By this time, we were all hungry and decided to go to a nice restaurant not too far from the house.

My mouth was salivating as I read the menu. Filipino food is one of the tastiest foods you'll ever eat. They had all my favorite dishes and desserts! All the food was delicious, and my new family was perfect. As we ate together as a family, I felt complete, incredibly blessed, and on top of the world. As with many cultures, the dinner table is a common gathering place. This is where the best foods are served, and the most intimate conversations are made. Memories and bonds are built and strengthened at the gathering table. Just as Jesus did throughout the Bible, whether he fed the thousands or His disciples at His last supper, it was around food and heart-to-heart conversations, food for the soul.

Later that evening, they asked for me to sleep over so we would have time to talk more. I was hesitant because I didn't have any of my clothes and things with me. It was all still at my godmother's house. So, they decided that I should go to my godmother's house, pack my things, and sleep there; then they would pick me up the next day. I left that night happy and fulfilled. I could not wait to spend the rest of my vacation with my papa and my new family.

I thought everything had gone great—but the next morning did not go as planned. I was packed up and ready to go. My Ninang Arianne tried calling my sister Rachelle to see what time they were going to pick me up but got no answer. Hours passed, and there was still no answer, no call back. We tried to reach them every way we knew how. We even called Tita Servidea to ask her to help reach out, but no one returned our calls. Several messages were left, and at this point, I was worried something bad happened overnight. Turns out, I was right.

When Rachelle finally returned our calls, the news was disturbing. I suppose after all the dust settled and the excitement dissipated, my stepmom, Tita Betty, had time to really reflect on what had just happened, and she was furious. Thoughts of the past crept back into her mind and into her heart. Feelings of anger toward my papa resurfaced, the pain of his infidelity flooded her mind and broke her heart all over again. She realized that she was trapped and had no say in the situation. She remembered how she felt when she first heard about me, the secret child. The lies, the deceitfulness, it all rushed back to her and consumed her thoughts like a raging fire. It was bad. They had fought that night again.

My stepmom, whom I thought was fine with my presence, really wasn't. She had given everyone the impression that she and I were fine, but in reality, she had just been engrossed in the moment. She did not want me back in her house — period. I felt bad that Rachelle had to be in the middle of all of this. She was our go-between. We didn't want to rock the boat too much either, because of my papa's recent heart surgery. Stress was not good for him. Rachelle said it wasn't a good idea for me to visit them again, but Ninang insisted that I have the opportunity to spend time with my papa. This back and forth continued, until later that evening, when Zoe drove me back to my papa's house, regardless of Tita Betty's feelings. When we arrived, Zoe dropped me off and went on her way. I guess she didn't want to stay around long enough to see the fireworks.

I hesitated to walk to the front door. I was a little bit afraid of being there all by myself. I wasn't sure what to expect from my stepmom—we had, after all, disregarded her demands. I wasn't sure if she was expecting me or not, but either way, she had no say in the matter at that point. Especially after Papa and his siblings had already spoken to her. It's a respect thing to follow what the eldest sibling (Tita Servidea) asks of you, whether you like the decision or not. It is a big part of Filipino culture. Young people are expected to show respect to the elderly as well as older members of the family. It is customary to show respect to their elders at all times, especially if a request has been made. Although the request is taken as a command. Filipinos are known for having strong and close family ties. They place high regard and put importance on their family before anything else. This includes feelings; family is family period.

As I approached, she opened the door to let me in. She was quiet as she showed me to her bedroom—this was where she wanted me to sleep because it was the only room with air conditioning. After I got settled in, we all went out for dinner near the house at a different restaurant. It was me, my papa, Tita Betty, Rachelle, and her husband, Leo. It was a nice, quaint little place, and the food was delicious as well! At first, it was awkward, but then we started talking and tensions subsided. I'm sure that God was right there with my family that night as we ate dinner, talked, and spent time getting to know one another after such a long time apart. Afterward, we went back home, rested, and went to sleep. There wasn't much talking that night.

Tita Servidea called and left a message that night. She wanted to know if I was ok, and she was worried for me. The next morning, my older sister, Cathy, came home from her business trip. We ate breakfast together and got to know more about each other. The atmosphere changed a little. It was less tense. We all started relaxing around each other a bit more. I called my Tita Servidea and told her that everything was fine. We were all getting along. She was very happy for me.

As my final few days in the Philippines approached, my time with my new family was so valuable to me. We were able to spend some decent quality time together. We went to the malls and explored various places and ate at so many different restaurants. I was able to get to know each member of my long-lost family. I also got permission to call my stepmom, from Tita Betty to now Mama Betty. My Mama Betty and I were able to spend a day together, just me and her. It was nice — she made me feel like I was her daughter. We rode the jeepney to a nearby market. Then we walked around and stopped at a fruit stand. She asked me if I wanted anything. I said "No, thank you."

We continued on by foot. She held my hand so I would not get lost in the crowd, just like a mother would with her child. There were so many people just walking around on the street lined with fruit stands and various little markets called "Sari Sari," which means "various or assorted items." We approached a mall; it was smaller than the other ones we had visited prior. We both noticed a boba stand ahead as we entered in. We looked at each other and smiled. We went to the counter and ordered our boba drinks. We were quite thirsty at that point. We had a good bonding time together. It was so memorable to be able to spend time with your family that you have been missing for over 40 years. It was during this time that I was reminded that God restores all things. Deuteronomy 30:3 reads, "Your God will restore everything you lost; he'll have compassion on you; he'll come back and pick up the pieces from all the places where you were scattered."

I was to head back home to Pittsburgh on December 10, 2017. I was excited to see my hubby and children and be in my own house again. Three weeks without being with my own family was too long. But my inner child didn't want to go home. The little girl that was finally reunited with her papa and new family after over 40 years wanted to live that life she had missed out on. I was enjoying being with them, having the time of my life. Everything was new; I felt like a kid in a candy store. I was only 4 years old when I had first left the Philippines. There was still so much to see and do, so much to talk about and learn from each other. I did not want to leave my newfound family, especially my papa, the one who said that he loved me and that he's always loved me. My inner child did not want it to end.

The feeling of a parent's love and acceptance toward a child is a feeling like none other. Children, young and old, crave the feeling of being loved and to know that they matter in this world. That's all I had ever wanted as a child: genuine love and

94

acceptance from my parents. We were at the airport when reality hit me. Overflowing with tears, we said our goodbyes. We knew that it wasn't the last time we'd see or communicate with each other now that we were family. The 22-hour flight home was a lonely one. I felt so much sadness and joy all at the same time. I was sad that I had to leave my family that I just reunited with, but joyful that I knew we would see each other again. And I was happy to be coming home to see my hubby and children. Three weeks across the globe felt more like three months. Yes, I was happy to be coming home.

The sun was rising as we flew over the Pacific Ocean. Gazing out the window, I was admiring the beauty of God's vast creation. I thanked God for making my trip possible when the beauty of His plan dawned on me. At the beginning of this journey, there were so many obstacles and hurdles. I believed that the enemy was trying to put something in my way to prevent me from going to the Philippines, and I said that God must have a bigger plan. I've heard it said, "The bigger the attack, the greater the outcome." Well, God showed off, and what an extraordinary plan He had. God's plan was not only to reunite father and daughter but to reunite and restore the entire family.

Through the help of Facebook, the cousins who had been torn apart over four decades ago due to tragic circumstances were now getting reacquainted. Some continue to visit each other when in the Philippines or the United States. The enemy's number one way to ruin lives is to break families apart. He loves nothing more than to rob us of what is precious to us, demolish every being, and annihilate what is being made before it is made. What the enemy thought he could destroy and tear apart, God restored.

Prayer

God, I want to use my time to give You honor and praise.

You have done incredible things in my life

And the lives of those around me.

One day, all people will know of

Your power and glory.

Until then, please help me to live

In such a way that draws people to You.

In Jesus' name, Amen.

Chapter 13: Tying Loose Ends

Do you recall when I mentioned earlier that my parents, the ones I call my "mom" and "dad"—but who are actually my biological aunt and uncle—and I were estranged for three years due to a missed Father's Day phone call? Well, in November 2018, my family celebrated my grandmother's 95th birthday. Little did we know that this would be the last birthday of hers that we would celebrate together. My Lola ("grandmother") passed away the following year, May 11th, 2019.

All the families that could attend the birthday celebration flew from all over the United States to Chicago. I had not spoken to my estranged parents for years, but I knew that they were going to be there. I prayed about what I would say or do when I saw them. I instructed my children to greet them kindly and with the proper Filipino tradition of "mano po." The word *mano* is Spanish for *hand,* while the word *po* is often used in Filipino culture and language at the end of each sentence as a sign of respect when addressing someone older. Put together, *mano po* literally translates to *(your) hand please* as the greeting initiated by gently taking the elders hand to the young's forehead and saying the phrase *mano po* simultaneously. "Mano Po" is an endearing Filipino gesture of respect given to elders and as a way of accepting a blessing from the elder. It signifies good manners and bridges affinity between different generations.

I told my children that the past is in the past and to forgive them and move on. I had to remind myself of this as well. I didn't know what to expect when we saw them, or how they would react.

Much prayer went into this, as the following evening was the event. We were all dressed nicely and made our way to the hotel where the function was going to be, we greeted all the grandparents, aunts, uncles, cousins, nieces, and nephews, and everyone we passed by. Then we saw my parents—I still refer to them as that because they will always be my parents—Linda and Carlos.

The kids greeted them with "mano po." We all said "hi" and hugged each other, as if no time had passed. My children did what they were supposed to do, and they gave their hugs as well. My parents commented on how tall and beautiful the kids were getting. We chatted for a while. Conversations were good; there were no obvious feelings of hurt or regret. We all seemed to have moved on from our past hurts. What the enemy meant for evil, God turned it around for good, once again.

Prayer

God, just as You have forgiven me unconditionally,

You are asking me to forgive others.

Please help me to do that.

Fill me with humility and empathy

And help me to see other people

The way that You see them.

Show me how to love people the way that You do.

In Jesus' name, Amen.

Chapter 14: Forgiveness and Restoration

Deuteronomy 30:3 says, "Then the Lord your God will restore your fortunes. He will have mercy on you and gather you back from all the nations where he has scattered you." I love how gracious and good God's Word is. This portion of scripture was true in the past for the Israelites and is still true for us today. If you are estranged from a friend or a loved one, or if something was taken away from you, I encourage you to reach out to God and pray for the promises that He already established for you long ago. Then take that bold leap of faith and take back what the enemy took from you. Reach out to your loved ones and let them know how much you care for and love them. How much you've missed them.

You might be thinking, "But I can't do that," or "There's too much pain," or "They won't listen." If anyone knows what you're going through, it's me. Everything is going to be alright. Whatever the excuse is, let it go and let God work in you and through you, and He will take care of the rest. Per Romans 8:28, I believe that God causes everything to work together for the good of those who love Him, for His glory. If the other parties are not receptive, don't worry about it, you just do your part and keep reaching out and praying for your loved ones. God WILL restore all things, all relationships, in His perfect timing. "He who was seated on the throne said, 'I am making everything new!'" (Revelation 21:5)

Maya Angelou once said, "Love is a condition in the healing spirit so profound that it allows us to forgive. Love recognizes no barriers. It jumps hurdles, leaps fences, penetrates walls to arrive at its destination full of hope." That resonates with me. What about you? Stop and think about it for a minute. Love. Conquers. All. With God, we can forgive, hope, and love again. I know I couldn't have done that on my own, forgive someone who hurt me deeply. Forgiveness is not easy; it is painful. But unforgiveness has its own set of pains and will keep you in bondage.

I heard a preacher once give this illustration: as Jesus was hanging on the cross, nails in the palms of His left and right hand, and an even longer nail punctured through His feet. Limp, the weight of His body pulled down on His diaphragm. Jesus needed to push up on the nails in His feet, causing more pain so he could inhale and exhale, so He could speak. One of the last 7 phrases Jesus spoke, inhaling deeply, was, "Forgive them, for they know not what they do." It is painful to forgive. It is painful to carry sin. It is weighty, it hurts. God requires us to forgive. It's not optional. People say that you can choose to forgive or not. No, it's actually mandatory.

Forgive the people who have done things to you that were totally unfair and totally unjust. You might be wondering, where does it say that? The word "forgive" appears 127 times throughout the books of the Bible. Two scriptures that stand out to me are Ephesians 4:32 "Be kind and compassionate to one another, forgiving each other, just as in Christ, God forgave you." And Matthew 6:14-15 "Jesus said, 'If you forgive those who sin against you, your heavenly Father will forgive you. But if you refuse to forgive others, your Father will not forgive your sins." We are required to forgive endlessly, and it must come from your heart. We must forgive people so we can love people.

Honestly, it's a very difficult task when you're trying to do it all on your own. Your mind will always bring you back to the hurts, to the pain you endured. I'll let you in on a little secret... WITH GOD all things are possible. He can and He will restore you and everything that was stolen or taken away from you, when you release your anger, your bitterness, your problems, and your pain to Him. God is not obligated to heal the wounds you don't give Him.

Remember, forgiveness is not for anyone else but you. You do it so you can be free from the chains of the grudge or hurt that may be holding you back. It does not absolve the person who hurt you, but it frees *you* from the pain. It allows *you* to better your life and to better yourself. No one else can or will do it for you. If you need to forgive someone, make that first step, I'll be right here cheering you on! If you're not ready yet, no worries; it's an open invitation. When you find yourself trying this or that to fulfill that empty or missing feeling, but nothing seems to satisfy, come back to forgiveness, and give yourself an opportunity to live a fulfilling life.

If you got lost in my story, allow me to tie it all together for you once again. When the enemy made me feel ashamed of having no parents to call my own, God turned that situation around. He's the God of abundance. In fact, He gave me three sets of parents who love, accept, and treat me well. Not only me, but they also dote on my hubby and my children too. The enemy wanted me to believe in the lies that "I was a mistake" or that "I didn't matter." God showed me the truth and said, "No, I chose you, and you were made for more." The story the enemy wanted to paint for my life was a story of tragedy: rape, lies, and abuse. BUT GOD! Oh, but my God, my God had a different picture in mind. He turned my story into a story of hope, love, and restoration. The biblical meaning of the word "restoration" is to receive back *more* than has been lost to the point where the final state is greater than the original condition. God restored my family tree beyond measure.

God was working all things for my good, throughout the valley experiences as well as the peak experiences. They were all *life-giving* experiences. Through my deepest dark valleys, He gave me a new outlook on life. God purposed me. He rejuvenated my joy of living and my desire to live a full life. In my timidity, He reinstated my confidence and helped me believe that I can accomplish anything with Him by my side. God restores all things and redeems all things. And through my peak experiences, He recovered a longing in my heart.

Someone once told me that I was the bridge between the gap, which brought the families back together, to restore hope where hope was lost. And love conquers all. My family was given a second chance in life to be reunited with one another. God breathed life into the peaks and valleys of my existence. Because the enemy tried to destroy everything from me, God restored it all through my children. Even the things that I missed out on growing up, God redeemed and instilled in my sweet kids. All five of my children are healthy, intelligent, athletic, speak different languages, play various instruments, and are extremely talented, but most of all, they love and live for Jesus Christ. I am not merely bragging about my children, but I'm bragging about the goodness and faithfulness of God.

Repeatedly throughout the Bible, God blesses people for their faith and hardships by making up for their losses and giving them more than they previously had before. God not only promises to restore what was lost, but to restore it more abundantly. I felt His closeness and presence throughout this journey. He not only saved me, but He also restored my life. God was protecting me from myself and along the way showed me that I was worth something, that I was priceless in His eyes. God showed me that He will use anyone to fulfill His plans for the kingdom, regardless of our qualifications or our past, because He qualifies us, and our past is forgiven and forgotten in the sea of forgetfulness. God gave me meaning and purpose to live on and He gave me a platform to tell the world of His loving grace and mercy. God is so good! I pray that you believe it too!

Prayer

God, thank You for choosing to forgive me.

I don't deserve Your forgiveness,

But I know You are good and loving.

I want to be like You, and because You have forgiven me,

I want to forgive others.

Help me each day to remember

Your gift of forgiveness

And release my anger towards

Those who have wronged me.

In Jesus' name, Amen.

Chapter 15: Labels and Lies

"It turns out, believing lies that you're not enough, your story doesn't matter, and there's no way for you to make an impact... *that's how not to save the world.*"

- Hosanna Wong[3]

There are so many negative voices out there vying for our attention that we give them front row tickets to sit comfortably in our minds. Voices that come at us from family, spouses, friends, social media, the enemy, and even our own negative self-talk. Coming from all directions, we begin to wear those labels. Believe in those lies. When you give space to them, they take root. Slowly your identity is lost, until you forget who you truly are. Can you relate?

I believed so many lies throughout my life that in some areas, they came true. I was told that I was stupid, insignificant, and that I would not amount to anything. So, I started to believe the lies. I would get by in school; I never really liked to study, because the label of, "I'm not smart enough," had already taken its place, rooted in my mind. My "studying" would consist of cramming at the very last minute. Although I would get decent grades, it really wasn't the best way to learn. I wasn't a bad student; I was just told repeatedly that I wasn't

---

[3] https://www.hosannawong.com/savetheworld

good enough, and I started to believe in it. I never finished college (*shhhh*, don't tell anyone). I wanted to, but couldn't and didn't believe in myself, that I could do it. The voices in my head echoed my mom's voice, it kept telling me that I wasn't going to amount to anything anyway, that I wasn't going to make an impact.

I completed my associate of applied science degree but wasn't proud of it. Truth be told, I was embarrassed that that's all I had to show for my work, but I at least finished halfway, right? Wrong! I should've been proud of myself for accomplishing something. I continued my college education for another year or so, but then dropped out because I didn't believe that I could go further and graduate with a bachelor's degree. That felt unattainable. I didn't think I deserved it. After all, my parents were never proud of me, so how could I be proud of myself? These lies that had been ingrained in my mind were just that: LIES! Wow, how the enemy's favorite pastime is to fill what's between our ears with negativity. He loves to get in our brain and fill it with doubt and discouragement, and then whispers…

This. Is. YOU!

He whispers it, but it resonates loudly in our heads and starts to overtake our hearts. The lies become truths; then with the false truths, we become insecure… insecure of who we truly are. Our identity is often stolen. But this was never God's intention for His children. We must claim victory over our minds, victory over our identities, and victory over our fears and doubts. Isaiah 41:10 says, "Do not fear, for I am with you; I will strengthen you and uphold you with My righteous right hand." We are made victorious in Christ Jesus!

Prayer

God, my life is Yours.

Please take every part of it.

Every area of my life that doesn't honor You–

Take it.

Every insecurity, fear, selfish ambition, and past hurt–

I give it all to You.

Please put those things to death

So that way I can experience Your abundant life.

In Jesus' name, Amen.

Chapter 16: Dreams Do Come True

Thanks to the courage I gained from my personal story, from reuniting with my family and mending the bond between the two sides, I started to believe in myself. I looked to God again for a goal that was on my heart and prayed.

On April 30th, 2021, the pastors at my church, Champion Christian Center, announced that they were going to launch Champion Leadership Academy (CLA) that fall. CLA is an accredited ministry school that is a member of Transworld Accrediting Commission International. Transworld has been around for 35 years and has established high standards of excellence and shared biblical doctrine. CLA was created to encourage world-class leaders to leave an impact on their generation, equipping and empowering them toward what God has called them to do.

This was an exciting announcement and I wanted to be a part of it. I knew that God had called me to be more and do more, but I wasn't sure what that was and how I was going to do it. Then, doubt and fear started to set in my mind again. Going back to school in my late 40s, I didn't think I could do it. This would be a three-year commitment. Completion of the first year would render a ministry certification, the second year a ministry license, and the third and final year ministry ordination. I thought that if I could do this, then I could prove to myself and others that I am smart and that my belief about me being a failure and not amounting to anything would finally become a lie.

I didn't mention to anyone, not even my family, that I was interested in taking classes, because I was afraid of what they might say. So, I prayed about it. Time passed, and before I knew it, they announced the last call for CLA fall registration. I prayed again and asked God to make a way to pay for the schooling, as well as to give me the confidence to do it well. An encouraging quote from my pastor echoed in my heart. She said, "If it's His will, it's His bill!" As Psalms 37:4 mentions, "Delight yourself in the LORD, And He will give you the desires *and* petitions of your heart." And so, on August 24th, I received my acceptance letter to attend Champion Leadership Academy. God made a way when I thought there was no way, and He paid it all in full! Thank you, Jesus! The first official day of class was September 7, 2021.

I remember sitting in class with my friends, thinking, *I'm the second oldest one here; I must keep up with these youngsters and I must make better grades than them.* I didn't want to expose my (perceived) lack of intelligence or the fact that I never finished college. I didn't have that validation. I felt like I had to prove it to myself, to someone, anyone. I recall a scene at the end of the movie *Creed II*, where Adonis Creed was sitting in his corner, eye swollen shut and worn out. Rocky Balboa pleads with him to throw in the towel, because he has nothing to prove to anyone. Creed's response: "I have to prove that I wasn't a mistake." He steps back into the ring with the true heart of a fighter and wins the title.

I was fighting for that title.

The first week of class, I was hyper-focused and studying so hard that I started to panic and was terrified. I started to believe that I wasn't going to make it and that I was going to fail school again. The thought of just dropping out opened a door to escape. It was only the first week! It's okay; people would just think that I was too busy with five kids, or the timing wasn't right. An outpouring of insecurities came rushing back into my head, reminding me of the lies that I once believed were truth. Then God quickened me to read Isaiah 43:18-19:

"Forget the former things; do not dwell on the past.

See, I am doing a new thing!

Now it springs up; do you not perceive it?

I am making a way in the wilderness and streams in the wasteland."

Not only did God make a way, but He also gave me a clean slate and believed that I could do it. He believed in me so I was able to believe in myself. Able to be confident in myself and remember my past no more. I was made new. I was made whole. My mind was renewed in Christ. I took a deep breath, and from then on, I made a promise to God that I was doing this for Him and for me. No one else's opinion or comments mattered, whether good or bad. It was all for God's glory to equip me and prepare me for what He has in store for me to do. An audience of One.

A big part of these classes was reading, researching, and writing papers, lots of papers. I remember asking my husband to read over some of my papers to see what his thoughts were on them. He would comment, "You wrote these? I didn't realize you could write so well." My first thought was that even my own husband doubted my intellectual abilities. Then I recalled that he had never read anything I wrote that was longer than an email, and his compliment fueled my fire.

When I completed the first year of ministry school, one of my classmates told me that he heard I was top of my class. I never did confirm this, but nonetheless, I did my best, and I did it all for the glory of God. On graduation day in May of 2022, I stood before my family, my pastors, my instructors, and the entire congregation, walked across that platform, and received my ministry certificate! This was truly an honor and an accomplishment for me. To make the day more special and a double blessing, my hubby, Chuck, was able to transfer his credentials over to CLA, and he too received his official ministry license.

I started year two of CLA in August of 2022. It was even more challenging, but I was no longer afraid or had doubts in my mind about my abilities. I knew then (and know now) that I am anointed to do hard things, and with God by my side and the Holy Spirit's direction, I will complete my goals. On June 4, 2023, I graduated and walked across the platform once again in front of my family, friends, pastors, instructors, and the congregation, and received my ministry license! Around the same time, I also became a published author with this book to help others discover their God-given purpose to do what they are created and called to do. These are huge achievements and major accomplishments for me.

Then God willing, in the fall of 2023, I will start my final year of ministry school so I can graduate and receive my ministry ordination—the icing on the cake. Whatever God has next for me, I will be obedient to the call. The enemy will always try to deter and disrupt you, but never give up and never give in.

Psalms 32:8 in the Amplified version the Lord says, "I will instruct you and teach you in the way you should go; I will counsel you [who are willing to learn] with my eye upon you." Before the existence of CLA, God was grooming and equipping me in many areas of ministry. For over 12 years, a ministry that I've been involved with and that I hold very near and dear to my heart is Beyond Survival Ministry (BSM). I started as a volunteer, but now I am a part of their core team and hold the position of BSM/Arise donations coordinator. I was able to participate in A Time to Heal Beyond Survival small group, which helped me identify the truth of God's Word and separate the lies the enemy had me believing. The invaluable information that I received allowed me to heal from my past.

Beyond Survival Ministries (BSM) is a 501(c)(3) non-profit, Christian organization dedicated to ministering to the needs of countless men, women, and families by restoring hope and transforming lives not only in our local community, but also across the United States, and abroad. We address many of life's challenging issues through professional Christian counseling, coaching, small group ministries, outreaches, conferences, retreats, workshops, leader trainings and now the Beyond Survival Ministries Podcast. Rev. Sue Willis—I call her my *Mentor Mama*—is the founder and executive director of BSM. I am a certified leader for A Time to Heal Beyond Survival (ATTHBS), Kingdom Girls, and Save One groups. In the fall of 2023, I will take part in the Daughters Arising, mentoring initiative with Pastor Sue.

At my church, Champion Christian Center, I serve in many areas of our Dream Team. I serve as a Relay teacher for Ultra Kids Ministry, teaching the love of Jesus Christ to children 4 years old to kindergarten. I am part of the Merch team, Next Steps team, Awaken core team, and hospitality team for Elle Woman's Ministry. I am also the Manna Ministry coordinator as well as the donations coordinator for our outreach programs. I am a CLA-certified and -licensed minister. I am known as "Mama Logan" to several youths and youth groups that I've had the privilege of chaperoning and volunteering with. I have also had the honor of serving at many revival services as well as community outreaches and feeding the homeless. I am an ambassador for Christ. The hands and feet of Jesus. Giving honor and glory to God, forever and ever. Amen.

Prayer

God, without You, I am nothing.

All of my life belongs to You alone,

And so, I ask that You would use my life for Your glory.

Set me apart to do the good works

You have planned in advance for me.

Change the way I think and the way I live.

Draw me closer to You,

And remind me of Your unfailing love.

In Jesus' name, Amen.

THE UNRAVELING

Chapter 17: Our True Identity

I am thankful that I made a conscious and intentional decision to stop believing in the lies set forth by the enemy, because I was born for such a time as this.

I recently read an excellent book for one of my CLA courses entitled *Strengthening the Soul of Your Leadership: Seeking God in the Crucible of Ministry* by Ruth Haley Barton. Chapter 5 in her book, "The Conundrum of Calling," really spoke to me! I can relate to Moses throughout this chapter, from the beginning of his identity to the calling God had on his life. Barton writes, "I know the question about your identity has been a little confusing for you, but I have always known who you are." God has always known me. Regardless of my how I came to be, regardless of who raised me, regardless of my past, He knew me. "Now that you know who you are, I am calling you to do something out of the essence of your being." Because of my past, He is now calling me to do something out of the essence of my being. To tell my testimony and give hope to the hopeless.

"Every single thing that didn't make sense when it happened, that seemed too harsh or too random or too shameful, now finds its place in the storyline that brought us here." Wow! This is exactly the story of my life! One of my favorite verses in the Bible comes from Genesis 50:20, "You intended to harm me, but God intended it for good to accomplish what is now being done, the saving of many lives." Another passage that Barton wrote, "The people will follow you because you have met me. That is what qualifies you." I've often questioned whether my qualifications were sufficient. In Colossians 1:12, it tells me, "The Father, who has qualified you to share in the inheritance of His holy people in the kingdom of light." This next quote from Barton convinces me that I am qualified, "It is all about you (because you are the one, I have called) and it's not about you at all (because it was all about Me and My work in and through you)." And "This is yours to do, you are to speak My words." I believe it is my assignment, my calling to write my story of what God has done in my life and my families' lives. To speak His words and give hope to others. This entire chapter really excited and encouraged me to know that I'm walking in my calling. Ever since I was formed in my mother's womb, my calling was woven into the very fabric of my being. Who God created me to be and encompasses who I am.

Do you know who God says you are? I tell you the truth, it is written all throughout the Bible. How He created you so carefully and delicately. I have learned from my past that it does not matter how you came to be or where you came from or what you've been through. That's not your story, it doesn't have to be. Your past does not have the authority to dictate your future. You have the power to continue and rewrite your story with God's truth. My pastor would always say, "If you're not dead, then your story is not done." Another pastor said, "Don't put a period where God puts a comma... your story is not done yet." Pastor Robert Morris says this, "For every truth of God, Satan tries to offer a distorted counterfeit." Pay close attention to the labels you give permission to be placed on you.

I want to remind you in case you've forgotten or if no one has ever told you about your true identity. God is calling you. This is who He says you are, and the enemy doesn't want you to know.

- You are **UNIQUE**—"You made all the delicate, inner parts of my body and knit me together in my mother's womb." (Psalms 139:13)
- You are **ENOUGH** & You are **MADE WHOLE**—"I praise you because I am *fearfully and wonderfully made*; your works are wonderful; I know that full well." (Psalms 139:14)
- You are **WORTHY**— "So don't be afraid; you are more valuable to God than a whole flock of sparrows." (Matthew 10:31)
- You are **FORGIVEN**—"For His unfailing love toward those who fear Him is as great as the height of the heavens above the earth. He has removed our sins as far from us as the east is from the west." (Psalms 103:11-12)
- You are **SPECIAL** & You are **BEAUTIFUL**—"For we are God's masterpiece. He has created us anew in Christ Jesus, so we can do the good things he planned for us long ago." (Ephesians 2:10)
- You are **LOVELY** & You are **INTELLIGENT**—"Those who are wise will shine as bright as the sky, and those who lead many to righteousness will shine like the stars forever." (Daniel 12:3)
- You are **PRECIOUS**—"You are precious in my eyes, and honored, and I love you." (Isaiah 43:4)

- You are **BELOVED**—"See what great love the Father has lavished on us, that we should be called children of God! And that is what we are! The reason the world does not know us is that it did not know Him." (1 John 3:1)
- You are **STRONG** & You are **VICTORIOUS**—"You have given me your shield of victory. Your right hand supports me; your help has made me great." (Psalms 18:35). And "But the Lord stood with me and gave me strength so that I might preach the Good News in its entirety for all the Gentiles to hear. And he rescued me from certain death." (2 Timothy 4:17)
- You are **FREE**—"So if the Son sets you free, you are truly free." (John 8:36)
- You are a **NEW CREATION**—"This means that anyone who belongs to Christ has become a new person. The old life is gone; a new life has begun!" (2 Corinthians 5:17)
- You are **CHOSEN**—"You didn't choose me, I chose you." (John 15:16) And "You are chosen, and you are His treasured possession." (Deuteronomy 7:6)

I overcame because of my faith, and now, I'm enjoying my reunited family and reaching for my goals, believing in myself, and watching my children grow into the amazing people God intended them to be.

Everyone has a story to tell. What's yours? You might not think it's important or significant. Or that it would have an impact on anyone at all. I used to think this way, and sometimes, I mistakenly allow the enemy to fool me. What I've learned is that the enemy will fill your head with all sorts of negative thoughts about how insignificant you are or insignificant your story is. The enemy continues to repeat, "What you went through is only yours; no one else is going through that." "You cannot influence or have an impact on anyone." "You are alone!" I want you to know that these are all lies and schemes from the devil. He doesn't want you to tell people your story, because then you will have a greater impact in your generation, throughout the world. You will turn people's hearts and minds away from sin and toward their Creator and Father, God.

The enemy knows this all too well, and that's why he would rather fill your time with other things, so you don't get your story out there. To distract you. Not everyone believes in God or Jesus, but they have at some point in their lives heard of Him. People sometimes equate the good things that happen in their lives to a "higher power" not realizing that that "higher power" is really, God the Father. We are all created from Him. Genesis 1:27 says, "God created man in His own image, in the image of God He created him." Go ahead, take that leap of faith, and tell your story. You matter. Someone out there, on the other side is waiting for your obedience, to give them the courage to tell their story. Help propel them and encourage them to tell theirs because they matter too.

We can learn from each other's experiences. As Proverbs 27:17 tells us, "People learn from one another, just as iron sharpens iron." We are all one body in Christ, with many different parts, but all are important to function properly. 1 Corinthians 12:25-27 says, "This makes harmony among the members, so that all the members care for each other. If one part suffers, all the parts suffer with it, and if one part is honored, all the parts are glad. All of you together are Christ's body, and each of you is a part of it."

There are billions of people in this world, and yes, someone out there has gone through a version of what you've gone through or what you're currently going through. But how will someone know the goodness of the Lord or what He's done for you if you don't share it? Romans 10:14 explains, "But how can they call on Him to save them unless they believe in Him? And how can they believe in Him if they have never heard about Him? And how can they hear about him unless someone tells them?" Share what you know to help and encourage one another, believer of God or not, we all need help, we all need encouragement. We all need to know that it's going to be ok. That there is hope, that there is love, and that God can turn situations around and He will restore all things for your good.

Let us be the ones to take that leap of faith and tell the world of our story. Let us overflow the nations with the goodness of God. "For as the waters fill the sea, the earth will be filled with an awareness of the glory of the Lord," (Habakkuk 2:14).

Is your story unraveling? Has God restored it back together? What has He done for you? How has He saved you and from what? We are to speak of His Word and give hope to others. Go tell someone of how God saved you and that they too can have that same freedom. I like how Ruth Haley Barton puts it, "Our transformation is never for ourselves alone. It is always for the sake of others." Jesus shines through us and touches a broken world in need of hope.

Prayer

God, I am so grateful that I get to be

A part of Your great story.

Thank You for having a plan

And a purpose for my life.

Help me not to step back in fear,

But to be able to step out in faith

And do what You've called me to do.

Remind me each day that I am enough for You,

And that You are enough for me.

In Jesus' name, Amen.

Epilogue: A Call to Salvation

Our God is a God of restoration. Our God is a God of love. From the beginning of time, our Creator only wanted to love and have a relationship with His creation, His people, His children. In Jeremiah 31:3 the LORD said, "I have loved you, my people, with an everlasting love. With unfailing love, I have drawn you to myself." God wants you. He's waiting for you to just reach out to Him. To just cry out to Him. Come as you are, and He will meet you right there. Just like the prodigal son that wanted to return to his father, you too can come boldly to your Heavenly Father. There's no need for you to get ready or be perfect, your Creator wants you just the way you are.

As my Pastor would say, if you don't know Jesus Christ, if you've never received Him into your life, or if you served Him but left the faith, you lived how you wanted to live. Today, you know that you need to surrender your life, fresh and new. If you find yourself in any of those places today where you need to surrender your life to Jesus, I want you to confess out loud.

Say:

God, today, I want to surrender my life to you. Heavenly Father, thank you for your son, Jesus. Thank you that He died and took my place. I ask you to forgive me of my sins, come into my heart, fill me with your Spirit. And from now on, I live for you, in Jesus' name. Amen.

Now if you've confessed with your mouth the prayer above and truly believed it in your heart (not just reading it, because you're in the middle of reading this book), I welcome you into the family of God! You are now a son or daughter of the most high God! Congratulations!

Please email me at judiloganministries@gmail.com and let me know. I'd love to send you a personal congratulations and a gift.

This is a special day for you. Be proud that you made the decision to live for God. You do not have to make a dramatic or drastic change unless you feel that nudge or tug from the Lord to do so. Right now, all you need to do is find a Bible-believing local church. Contact them and let them know that you've received Christ in your heart, and they will direct you from there. Remember, you are not doing this for anyone else but yourself, so you can be free from all the bondage and strongholds that are holding you back. Romans 8:1-2 says, "Therefore, there is now no condemnation for those who are in Christ Jesus, because through Christ Jesus the law of the Spirit who gives us life has set you free from the law of sin and death." And in John 8:36, "So if the Son sets you free, you will be free indeed." Choose life and be free!

Prayer

God, thank You for the great gift of salvation.

Thank You for the grace and mercy

That You've given to me.

Thank You for sending Jesus to make it possible

To have a relationship with You.

Help me live in gratitude of my salvation

Each and every day.

Show me ways that I can share this good news

With others in my life.

In Jesus' name, Amen.

Resources

National Suicide Prevention Lifeline 800.273.8255

www.988lifeline.org

For people in distress who feel like they are at risk of harming themselves.

Beyond Survival Ministries 888.868.3603

www.beyondsurvivalministries.org

Restoring hope and transforming lives of men and women who are suffering from emotional pain, trauma, and brokenness. A ministry of hope and healing for those who have suffered from the trauma of rape, sexual abuse, or sexual assault or who have been the victim of sex trafficking.

- Professional Christian counseling
- Coaching
- Small group ministries
- Outreach
- Conferences
- Retreats
- Workshops
- Leader trainings
- Podcast

SaveOne 615.636.2654

www.saveone.org

Helping men, women, and loved ones recover mentally, emotionally, and spiritually, after the choice of abortion.

Champion Leadership Academy (CLA) 724.916.4013

www.championacademy.co

A ministry school with excellence. A member of Transworld Accrediting Commission. Open to men and women who are interested in serving in Christian leadership. If you want to see your faith fueled, your calling defined, and your spirit on fire to see this generation changed by the power of the Gospel, call and enquire about enrollment.

About the Author

Judi Logan is a mother of five amazingly talented children. She lives in Bethel Park, PA with her husband, kids, and sweet Asha, their Aussiedoodle. Judi is a credentialed minister, serving at her church, revival meetings, and community outreaches throughout Pittsburgh and the surrounding areas. She uses her story of overcoming the challenges in her life to inspire others to love themselves, forgive others, and come to God.

Judi loves spending time with her family and friends. Going out to eat and discovering new restaurants is her favorite pastime. She loves taking pictures of food that makes your mouth salivate just looking at it and she especially loves to capture every moment and every person in her life that she encounters. Judi loves people, and once you meet her, you've made a friend for a lifetime.

Connect With Judi Logan

Website:

www.judilogan.com

On Facebook and Instagram:

@authorjudilogan

Email:

judiloganministries@gmail.com

To book Judi for a speaking event or to be a guest on your podcast, please contact her via email at judiloganministries@gmail.com.

Printed in the USA
CPSIA information can be obtained
at www.ICGtesting.com
LVHW020806221023
761201LV00012B/201